MW00475654

West Point
U.S. Military Academy

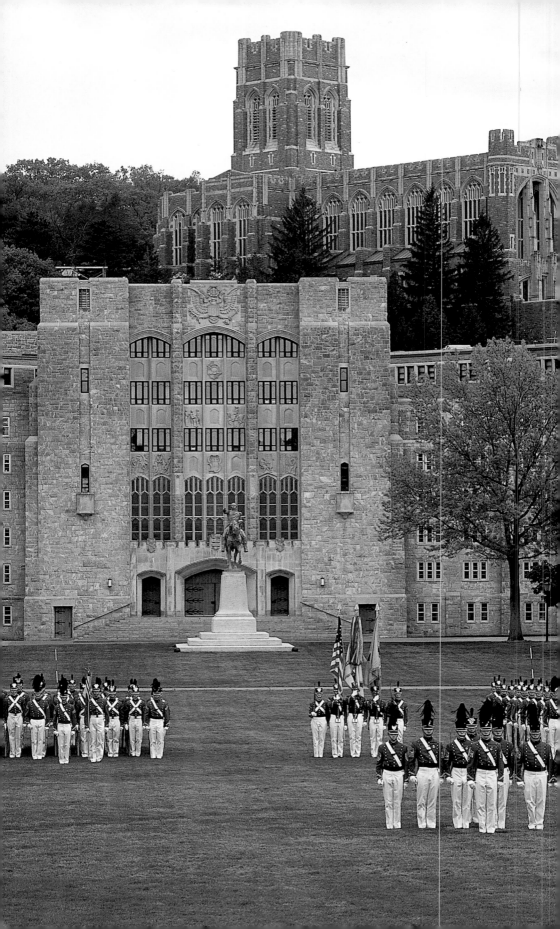

THE CAMPUS GUIDE

West Point
U.S. Military Academy

An Architectural Tour by
Rod Miller

Photographs by Richard Cheek

Foreword by Alexander M. Haig, Jr.

Princeton Architectural Press
NEW YORK | 2002

This book has been made possible through the generous support of the Graham Foundation for Advanced Studies in the Fine Arts.

Princeton Architectural Press
37 East 7th Street
New York, NY 10003

For a free catalog of books published by Princeton Architectural Press, call 1.800.722.6657 or visit www.papress.com

Series editor: Jan Cigliano
Series concept: Dennis Looney
Design: Sara Stemen
Layout: Mary-Neal Meador
Copy editor: Heather Ewing
Maps: Jane Garvie
Index: Andrew Rubenfeld

Special thanks to Nettie Aljian, Ann Alter, Amanda Atkins, Nicola Bednarek, Janet Behning, Megan Carey, Penny Chu, Tom Hutten, Clare Jacobson, Mark Lamster, Nancy Eklund Later, Linda Lee, Anne Nitschke, Evan Schoninger, Lottchen Shivers, Jennifer Thompson, and Deb Wood of Princeton Architectural Press
—Kevin C. Lippert, *publisher*

ISBN 1-56898-294-1

Cataloging-in-Publication Data is available through the Library of Congress

Printed in China

CONTENTS

How to use this book xiv

Foreword by Alexander M. Haig, Jr. xvi

Introduction to West Point 1

Walk 1 **Buffalo Soldiers Area** 10

Walk 2 **Academic Area** 28

Walk 3 **Chapel Area** 76

Walk 4 **Academy Housing and Enlisted Men's Area** 92

Walk 5 **Post Services Area** 112

Walk 6 **Monuments and Memorials** 128

Bibliography 141

Acknowledgments 143

Index 144

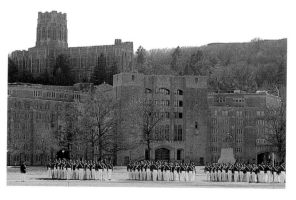

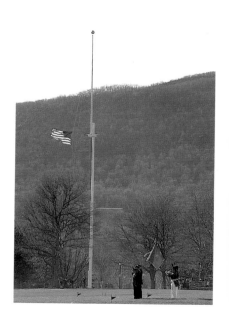

How to use this book

This *Campus Guide* is intended for visitors, alumni, and students who wish to learn more about the history and buildings of the United States Military Academy at West Point. West Point is a large campus, covering 16,000 acres and containing more than 1,400 structures. Just over sixty of the Academy's most notable buildings and sites are included in the guide, from the Plain and Olmsted Hall to Buffalo Soldiers' Field, Mahan and Taylor Halls, to the Cadet, Jewish, and Catholic Chapels. All these are beautifully situated along the banks of the Hudson River.

Following an overall introduction, the book is divided into six Walks covering the major campus areas: Buffalo Soldiers Area, Academic Area, Chapel Area, Academy Housing and Enlisted Men's Area, Post Services Area, and Monuments and Memorials. Each Walk is a separate chapter comprised of an introduction that describes the history of the area, with a map and a list of buildings on the Walk, followed by entries on each building. Photographs and details on dates and designers accompany the entries. Each building at the Academy has a clearly posted identification number. These same numbers are found in parenthesis with each building included in the text. (The other number for each building is given by the publisher to identify the building on the locator maps.)

There are many other places to see while visiting West Point. The large housing areas to the north and west of the campus reflect different eras of military base planning; the walking paths often offer dramatic views of the campus and the Hudson River; two Revolutionary War forts—Clinton and Putnam—provide interesting insight into this military era; and historical memorials commemorating wars and notable alumni are located throughout the grounds. Visitors are urged to schedule time for a leisurely visit to the cemetery behind the Cemetery Chapel.

A final note regarding the size of the campus. The breadth and rolling terrain make a walk through the entire campus a daunting endeavor; there are also few nearby public restroom facilities. The visitor may stumble upon a refreshing water fountain from time to time, many placed about the campus as memorials from individual classes. There are suggestions in the text about which areas to view on foot and which are more suitable to visit by automobile.

West Point Visitor's Center: 845.938.2638 email: 8visit@usma.edu
Open daily 9:00 am to 4:45 pm (except Thanksgiving, Christmas, and New
Year's Day)

West Point Museum email: museum@usma.edu
Open daily 10:30 am to 4:15 pm (except Thanksgiving, Christmas, and New
Year's Day)

Guide Bus Tour Information: 845.446.4724

Gift Shop: 845.446.3085

The USMA website has a schedule of guided tours around West Point.
www.usma.edu

A special note: The United State Military Academy at West Point
is unlike other schools of higher education. In addition to being a teaching
university, it is an active military base. Visiting here is different than an
afternoon strolling around Brown University, for example. Restricted areas
are not accessible by unescorted civilians and visitors are urged not to enter;
these areas are designated by small brown signs. A few buildings included in
the *Campus Guide* are located in these regions; please view these fine structures from surrounding buildings or atop the Cadet Chapel. Many other
buildings are also private and not open to visitors. Suggestions for viewing
and visiting particular buildings are offered in the text. Photography is permitted everywhere outdoors around the campus.

Foreword

The architecture of the United States Military Academy at West Point reflects the history, traditions, and strengths of the United States of America as well as the character of its armed forces. Originally chosen as a defense position against British forces during our nation's war for independence, West Point became a military academy in 1802. Since then, the architects of its facilities have adhered over the years to West Point's military mission, while effectively utilizing its rolling topography on the bluffs of the Hudson River.

Through the Gothic portals of the U.S. Military Academy our nation's finest have passed. For two hundred years, in war and peace, West Point graduates have served the vital interests of the United States and like-minded nations. Countless graduates of the Academy have gone on to illustrious careers as officers in the U.S. Armed Forces. From the War of 1812, through the opening of America's West, the Mexican War, Spanish-American War, World Wars I and II, the Korean War, Vietnam, Desert Storm, and in numerous other encounters, West Point graduates have proven to be among the world's finest military leaders. Sadly when our nation was torn asunder during the Civil War, West Point classmates, following their roots, took up sides, either serving with the Union or joining the Confederacy. When the war ended, members of the Long Gray Line contributed to the national healing process and brought unity once again through the Academy's Corps of Cadets.

As the Academy's founder Sylvanus Thayer envisioned, members of the Long Gray Line have also contributed to our nation's success in pursuits other than the military. West Pointers have been acclaimed for their contributions as artists, engineers, writers, physicians, astronauts, political leaders, ambassadors, investors, government advisors, cabinet officers, and corporate leaders. Their contributions to the well-being and quality of life of peoples around the world have marked a West Point education as the finest.

The Campus Guide: West Point, U.S. Military Academy, Rod Miller's architectural tour of West Point, with beautiful photographs by Richard Cheek, is a fitting tribute to the history of West Point and its graduates. It effectively brings to the public a great deal that is heretofore unknown. It is fortuitous and appropriate that this book is published during the celebration of West Point's Bicentennial. This two-hundred year anniversary connotes the U.S. joining symbolically, if not historically, those nations which have long since achieved maturity.

This publication focuses the reader not just on the bricks and mortar that make up the buildings. It provides a purposeful and meaningful history of the institution. A visit to West Point with this *Campus Guide* in hand will enrich the reader, not just in architectural design but the essence of what

Parade on the Plain

the U.S. Military Academy represents: its military traditions and the contributions of its graduates to our nation's security and well-being. West Point's architecture and landscape embodies the soul of our nation's heritage, its excellence in education and the patriotism of its graduates. Many who made the ultimate sacrifice chose West Point as their final resting place in a modest cemetary just off the West Point Plain overlooking the Hudson Valley.

Reading this book reawakens memories of my time spent at West Point, first as a cadet in the Class of 1947 and in subsequent years as a tactical officer, Regimental Commander, and Deputy Commandant, as well as my return visits as Deputy National Security Advisor, as NATO Commander, and as a private citizen and former member of the Board of Visitors. As the fifty-ninth Secretary of State, I am grateful for the unique character of the overall educational experience at the U.S. Military Academy. The broad aspects of the West Point educational program are singularly designed to prepare young men and women to command America's youth in time of war. In this respect, no other educational experience can match Service Academy training for its emphasis on physical development, intellectual rigor, self-discipline, and the attainment of a mature philosophical outlook. Admittedly, life as a cadet at West Point is taxing, challenging, and at times frustrating, but always rewarding and on occasion, even humorous.

The images of America's leaders grace the landscape of West Point. The names on buildings, statues, plaques, and portraits abound (Washington, Grant, Pershing, Sherman, Lee, Patton, Bradley, MacArthur, and Eisenhower) bringing to life for cadets, as well as visitors, the richness of our nation's history and the contributions of its graduates to this history.

It is the words of General Douglas MacArthur, Class of 1903, to the Corps, on May 12, 1962 from the "poop deck" of Washington Hall that best capture the meaning of the U.S. Military Academy to its graduates. Excerpted paragraphs from that historic speech read:

> You are the leaven which binds together the entire fabric of our national system of defense. From your ranks come the great captains who hold the nation's destiny in their hands the moment the war tocsin sounds. The Long Gray Line has never failed us. Were you to do so, a million ghosts in olive drab, in brown khaki, in blue and gray, would rise from their white crosses thundering those main words – *Duty – Honor – Country*.
>
> This does not mean that you are war mongers. On the contrary, the soldier, above all other people, prays for peace, for he must suffer and bear the deepest wounds and scars of war. But always in our ears, ring the ominous words of Plato, that wisest of all philosophers: "Only the dead have seen the end of war."

This is our U.S. Military Academy at West Point. May the reader of this guide be as inspired by the richness of West Point's architectural history as were those who passed through its halls, walked its grounds, and gone on to serve as defenders of America's freedom.

Alexander M. Haig, Jr.
West Point Class of 1947

Introduction to West Point

Situated about sixty miles north of New York City, along a particularly strategic bluff of the Hudson River, is the United States Military Academy. The location, selected originally for military reasons, has become a key part of shaping the Academy's built environment. From its earliest use as a military school, geography and environment have played a profound role in the

The point at first light

View up the Hudson River

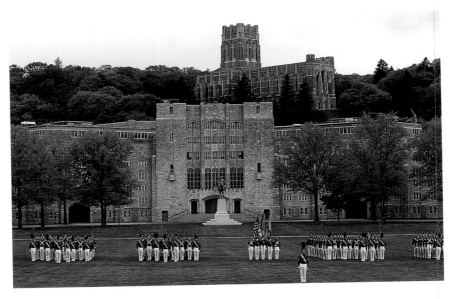

Parade on the Plain

organization of the campus. Buildings were sited in particular ways to take advantage, on a number of levels, of the natural features of the valley and bluff. In fact, as it developed, meaningful aspects of the Academy became about the *place*. Hill and river, stone and wall carry as much significance as heroes and legends. So much is the Academy about place that rarely is it referred to as the United States Military Academy, rather, it is called simply by its location: West Point.

Merely the name West Point conjures up romantic images of young cadets in smart wool uniforms, divisions of cadets marching in formation across the Plain, and giants of military and United States history: Grant, Pershing, MacArthur, Patton, Lee, Sherman. West Point is a place many know of yet few know about. How can it be that an institution that has produced so many men of stature, that has contributed so effectively to the memory of our nation can be so little known? This guide is an attempt to remedy that situation by providing information about the physical environment of the Academy. Architectural critic John Ruskin wrote, "without architecture we cannot remember." We would do well to remember, as the generations of architects who contributed to the Academy's physical fabric usually did so by aiming at the highest ideals and values of the nation.

A portion of those values was, and perhaps still is, wrapped up in the land. The area in which the Academy is situated, the Hudson River Valley, captivated many who encountered it. An entire school of artists was named after this place. Landscape painter Thomas Cole, most renowned of the school, was well known for his famous cycle, *The Voyage of Life*. He lived in Catskill. Another painter, Frederick Church, first gained acclaim for his vision of Niagara Falls, a painting that won a medal at the 1867 Paris Exposition. His home Olana, a Persian-inspired fantasy house, is in Hudson, New York. Artists came for the lush forests and stunning vistas of the river valley and its environs.

It was not merely the natural beauty of the place that was compelling in 1775. The Hudson River was recognized as an important avenue for communication along the northeastern section of the colonies. Both the British and the patriots wanted to control what went up and down and across the river. 1775 was the year when surveyors were sent out to choose the most strategic spot for fortifications. West Point was clearly it. At this point the river makes two turns, forcing ships to slow. Here, too, the river is

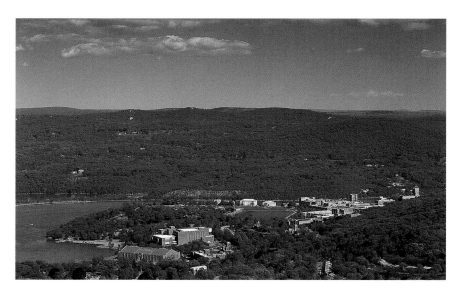

View of campus from Route 9W

Retreat review

narrower, creating rougher and more powerful currents. And, because of the narrowness, winds were tricky. Of course, above the river the bluff of the point emerges in such a way as to offer a very clear view up the river toward Newburgh and down the river. The bluff is also high enough above the river to provide a most profitable site from which to fire cannonballs at passing ships. By mid-1776 fortifications were constructed. After a shaky beginning, wherein the British briefly held the original forts, on January 27, 1778, patriot soldiers crossed over and camped on the western side of the river. West Point has not been without the army since.

No British army ever challenged West Point; no battles were fought there. The most excitement for the Point during the Revolution came in the form of an attempted betrayal. The American general Benedict Arnold, who had distinguished himself at the battles of Quebec and Saratoga, was given command of West Point in 1780. Feeling unappreciated by the country he had served so well, Arnold opened secret communications with the British in order to turn over to them the fortifications and garrison. The British hoped that his plan would bring a quick end to the war, and Arnold hoped for higher rank. Arnold's secret plans were revealed when British Major John André, with whom Arnold negotiated, was captured; and Arnold himself narrowly escaped arrest by the Americans. General Washington, commander-in-chief of the Continental army, recognized the immense strategic value of West Point and had it brought back up to standards (after Arnold's deliberate neglect).

West Point was kept on as a military base after the Revolutionary War, but it was not until 1790 that the young nation actually purchased the property (much to the relief of the owner, Stephen Moore, who had been waiting more than a decade for some sort of recompense). In 1795—with the temporary stationing here of the new Corps of Artillerists and Engineers—the first inkling that West Point might become something more than a fortress arose. In 1796 Washington suggested a permanent military academy. The lack of proper training on the part of the Continental army had been painfully obvious during the Revolutionary War. The formation of an academy was an idea long in the making.

A good deal of controversy was generated by the notion of an academy, not because it wasn't thought necessary but because of doubts of its constitutionality and fears of a separate, trained militia. Of course, it didn't help that with the Revolution now past, fears of further war were mostly alleviated. Various proposals and bills languished in Congress. It was not until 1800, after President Thomas Jefferson had been inaugurated, that the new Academy began to coalesce. Finally, in 1802 Jefferson signed into law the Military Peace Establishment Act. There is still debate as to exactly why Jefferson so quickly signed the act after opposing it during the Adams administration. Nevertheless, Jefferson signed and thus provided for, among other things, the recognition and support of a military academy. The United States Military Academy at West Point was officially founded.

The history of the Academy from its founding seems to follow a pattern paralleled by its architecture. At its founding the Academy consisted of a few spare buildings. The first structure selected as the Academy building was a two-story wooden building. By the time of the Academy's founding this building was already more than twenty years old. A few

Painting by George Catlin, c. 1828. Visible are the North Barracks, South Barracks, Academy, Cadet Mess, and Woods Monument. All of the buildings have been demolished and replaced.

houses, used as officers' quarters, were also present. It was not until around 1815 that buildings of a larger and more permanent nature were constructed. The most notable of these were the Cadet Mess, the Academy building, and the South and North Barracks. These simple buildings were arranged in much the same way in regard to the Plain as are the buildings today.

It is interesting to note that there exists a design plan for a "National Military Academy" that was drawn by Benjamin H. Latrobe, one of America's first professionally trained architects. Dated 1800 the plan was sent to President Jefferson, but it is unclear whether or not Jefferson actually saw it. It depicted a U-shaped academy building enclosing a central green space—a design that was considered more effective than the traditional, multistory rectangular block. While this central and orderly plan worked to good effect at the University of Virginia and Union College, it would have been disastrous for the Academy. The confines of West Point geography limit any successful addition to this sort of central plan.

The next notable period of building at the Academy began in 1836 with the construction of the Chapel. This happened under the superintendency of Major Richard Delafield (1838–45). Delafield's predecessor, Major Rene E. DeRussy, had approved plans for the Chapel designed in a simple Doric style. It is not clear if DeRussy had intended to continue in the Greek manner for other buildings, as Delafield replaced him before he had a chance to oversee more construction. Delafield, however, had some very clear notions about just what he wanted for the Academy. He set the stylistic tone, but not the style, for the future campus.

Exterior of Old Library, Delafield. Demolished in 1961.

View from Flirtation Point

When opportunity came for the Academy to build, Delafield was intimately involved. What struck him as the most appropriate style was something that has been labeled Tudor-Gothic. The buildings he designed— the Library, a barracks, and the Ordnance Compound—did, indeed, all share some elements of the same style: crenellation along the rooflines of the Library and barracks as well as the walls of the Ordnance Compound, para- peted towers on all three. Certainly Delafield was pleased with the visual effect of this style, but also with its historic significance. Elements of this style can be found in an odd assortment of English buildings ranging from the crenellated parapets and towers of Ely Cathedral (eleventh century) to the crenellated roofs of Bolsover Castle, Derbyshire (attributed to builder John Smythson, 1610) and those of St. John's College, Cambridge (1511). However, with Delafield's designs, while they do have these militaristic elements, they also shared some very traditional Gothic elements. His design for the Library contained regular fenestration, finials, and pointed arches with traceried windows. It is at this point that one realizes there is some confusion regarding the style, not just of Delafield's buildings but of many others.

One does not associate a military academy with delicate traceries or lofty vaulting but rather with thick walls, small windows, and a fortress appearance. In that sense the Academy's buildings are less Gothic and more Romanesque. Delafield's stripped down Gothic seemed to put later architects ill at ease. Richard Morris Hunt and Paul Philippe Cret, for example, didn't seem to be certain as to how to approach this Gothic tradition. Their buildings are rugged and less Gothic; they are masculine but somehow don't fit. (McKim, Mead & White circumvented the problem by designing classical structures that do not work.) What was needed was someone who understood the Gothic and Romanesque styles and their history and could make them work for the Academy. It took until the early twentieth century but the man whom the Academy got was the most knowledgeable Gothicist in America: Ralph Adams Cram.

It was Cram, Goodhue & Ferguson who, wisely taking their cue from the work of Delafield, developed a new style, a hybrid of various parts, historically and ideologically suited to a military academy. This style is not

Eisenhower, Old Central, Pershing, and Bradley Barracks, left to right

quite Romanesque, not quite Gothic, not quite Oxford—it is a simplified version of Gothic detail and massing with the rugged walls familiar to Romanesque and crenellations borrowed from Oxford. We might rightly refer to it as Military Gothic.

Military Gothic was the style Cram, Goodhue & Ferguson used in their entry for the 1903 competition and, due to the number of buildings that came from that competition, it was, and is, the defining style of the Academy. It is successful on many levels: the Gothic details echo the educational traditions of Oxford and Cambridge; the Gothic massing allows flexibility for the dramatic geography of West Point; the Romanesque walls tell of strength and courage; and the crenellations are a constant reminder of the Academy's military goals and history. This latter point is of no small measure, as the Academy is effective not only as a school but as a collective repository of military tradition. And this, of course, is vitally important to the functioning of a proper soldier; it is not the living warriors that make us take notice— rather, it is the dead who give us pause to contemplate the ideals for which we might fight and die—and those for which we may live.

Pre-1910 photograph shows the Plain (with draped cannons) in foreground and the Old Library (destroyed) and old Cadet Chapel (moved in 1910) in background. The buildings still follow this pattern, and today the new library is on the site formerly occupied by the Old Library.

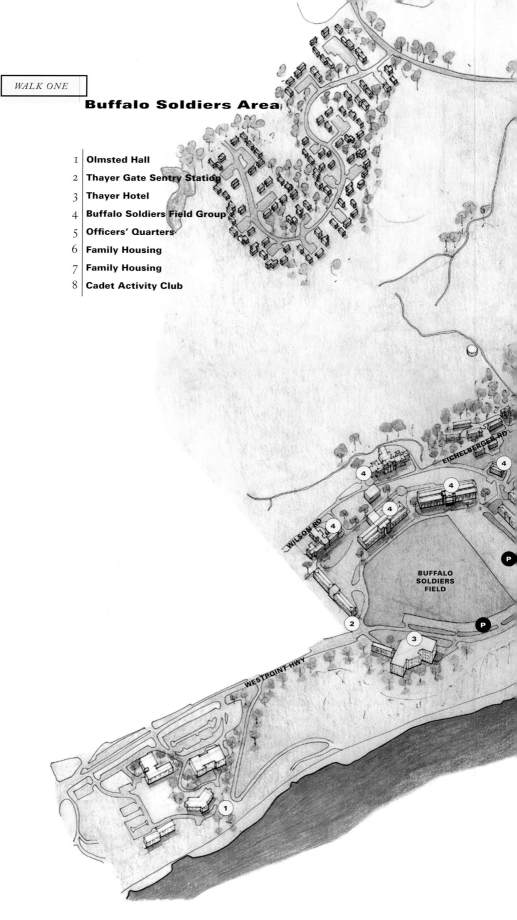

Buffalo Soldiers Area

1 | Olmsted Hall
2 | Thayer Gate Sentry Station
3 | Thayer Hotel
4 | Buffalo Soldiers Field Group
5 | Officers' Quarters
6 | Family Housing
7 | Family Housing
8 | Cadet Activity Club

EICHELBERGER RD

WILSON RD

BUFFALO
SOLDIERS
FIELD

WESTPOINT HWY

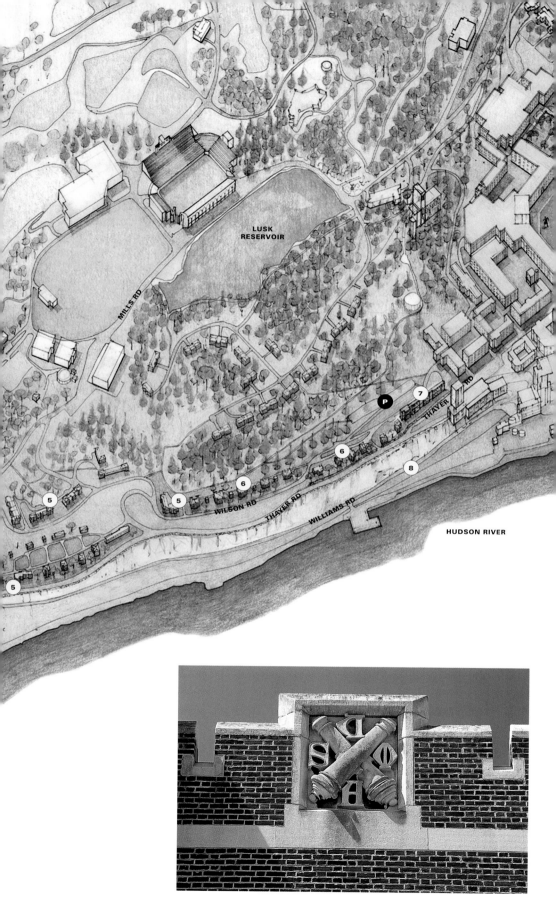

LUSK
RESERVOIR

MILLS RD

THAYER RD

P

7

6

6

8

5

5

5

5

WILSON RD

THAYER RD

WILLIAMS RD

HUDSON RIVER

This southern area of the West Point campus is relatively new. Unlike the older and more clearly established Academic Area and Plain, this portion of the acreage did not come into full use until the early twentieth century. It was planned as an area for cavalry and artillery drill. Equestrian skills were an essential part of military training for cadets. To aid them in acquiring such skills, the Academy hosted various cavalry regiments. One of the most famous of these, and the one for whom this area was named in 1976, was the Buffalo Soldiers. The Buffalo Soldiers were the legendary black cavalrymen who fought in the Spanish-American War alongside Theodore Roosevelt's Rough Riders and who kept the peace out west against Geronimo, Billy the Kid, and Pancho Villa. (They were also responsible for mapping areas of the Southwest and for stringing hundreds of miles of telegraph cable.) They were named "Buffalo Soldiers" by the Cheyenne and Comanche. In 1907 a detachment of these soldiers (from the 9th Regiment) was assigned to West Point to teach their skills to cadets. (In 1931 they were replaced by the 2nd Squadron of the 10th Cavalry.) Such training lasted until 1947 by which time it was clear that machinery was more effective in wartime than its equestrian counterparts.

This southern area of the campus was brought "in" with the rest of the campus when, in the late nineteenth century, the southern gate was moved much farther down Thayer Road. For many years this entrance was located higher up on Thayer Road (across from Quarters #8). (The original gate can still be seen at the entrance to the Old Cadet Chapel near the cemetery.) When moved, and a new and more expansive gate house built, there was more of a connection to the lower part of the campus as well as to the town of Highland Falls and, later, to Lady Cliff College.

With the new southern gatehouse, designed by Richard Morris Hunt, the stage was set to utilize the lower area. The 1903 competition winners, Cram, Goodhue & Ferguson, conceived of a special area for cavalry and artillery drill, surrounded by the requisite buildings. Inexplicably, their first location for the drill area was up on the northern end of the campus near the Enlisted Men's Hospital. Academy administrators disagreed with their choice of location and selected this southern end for three reasons: it was physically closer to the Riding Hall in the Academic Area; it was more sheltered from the blustery winds off the Hudson; and it provided a much more expansive area in which to practice drill maneuvers.

The administrators' decision to select this lower portion of the Academy was a good one. Thayer Road was settled along the scenic ridge and wound its way down toward Highland Falls. The Buffalo Soldiers area acts as a terminus for the entire campus. Depending upon which way one is traveling, the area may greet one with a scenic field, embraced by the large and handsome barracks and stables, foreshadowing the drama of the Academic Area buildings and Parade, or it may remind one upon departure of the real mission of the Academy, the training of soldiers.

1. Olmsted Hall (Pershing Center, #2110)

Architect unknown, 1937

The first building of note that greets the visitor to West Point is Olmsted Hall. Home to West Point's museum, also known as the Pershing Center, this building is behind the rather plain Visitor Center. These two, and the few other unremarkable buildings in this precinct, share a similar and rather sad history.

As the visitor will note, the buildings in this area are not located on the Academy campus proper. They are clearly separated from the southern Thayer Gate by a significant space and a McDonald's Restaurant (which also plays a part in the story). Originally this group of buildings formed the campus of Lady Cliff College. Lady Cliff College began as Ladycliff Academy, a private four-year Roman Catholic school for girls. It was opened in 1899 by the Franciscan Sisters of Peekskill. By all accounts the school was needed in the area and provided a good education for young women.

Ladycliff's history with the Academy was a pleasant one—at least when the Academy was not enduring growing pains. The young Ladycliff women often served as the dates of the young Academy men for the

Olmsted Hall

Academy formals. After Ladycliff Academy became Lady Cliff College, young men were admitted and thus even more children of Academy personnel joined the generations of those educated there. Of course being in such proximity to the Academy meant that the tiny college's campus was eyed eagerly when plans for expansion were discussed. In a number of reports of the board of visitors (the Academy's version of trustees) there was made mention of the desire to annex the college.

In the end, however, it was not the Academy that was responsible for closing down the college but mundane financial problems. Lady Cliff administrators announced to their faculty, one hour before announcing to the last graduating class, that 1980 would be its last year. The college was sold to the Academy for essentially the same amount as its debts; part of the deal, oddly, included a 1.6-acre tract of land upon which would be situated the neighboring McDonald's. In any case, it was the end of Lady Cliff but the beginning of another much needed expansion for the Academy.

By 1983 different groups from the Academy were vying for places in the "new" buildings. One of the first groups to get access, much to their relief, was the Visitor Center—which had been previously operating out of a decrepit section of a now demolished building near Buffalo Soldiers Field. The Lady Cliff library became their new home. It was the museum, however, that got the big prize: Rosary Hall. The building was renamed Olmsted Hall after Major General George H. Olmsted, a contributor to the museum.

This dramatic structure, once a classroom building, features angled wing halls flanking a center tower. The tower manages to at once anchor the wings and relieve what might otherwise be two regular, rectangular halls. The back of the building features a series of "set backs" and a semicircular patio, both of which sit upon a rusticated basement level. The building now houses the Pershing Center, the Academy's museum. The West Point Museum, first opened (elsewhere on campus) in 1854, is America's oldest and largest military museum.

2. Thayer Gate Sentry Station and Public Toilets (#610/608)

Office of the Quartermaster under Robert M. Littlejohn, #608, 1938; Roe-Eliseo, #610, 1988

Thayer Road provides the main course through the Academy's southern half of the campus. The bottom gate for this section was originally situated on Thayer across from Building #8, an officer's quarters. This tri-part, cast-iron gate was moved up to the cemetery and can still be seen at its entrance.

A new gate was needed and a design by Richard Morris Hunt, of around 1894, was approved lower down Thayer Road, where today's Sentry

Thayer Gate Sentry Station

Station now stands. Hunt's gatehouse was of a rugged, rusticated granite with small crenellated towers. It was a functional building that was similar to some of Hunt's other work on the campus. (Hunt's other building at the Academy is the Pershing Barracks #751 in Walk Two.)

Hunt's gatehouse was more than enough for the minor traffic coming to the Academy at the time. By 1909, however, motor vehicles required more space and Hunt's building was partly removed. A single pillar still stands next to the west side of the entrance. In 1938 a thoughtful quarter-master, Colonel Robert M. Littlejohn, realized the need for public facilities in this area and had them constructed just to the west of the gatehouse. After this addition it appears that the gate area was further modified in the 1940s for increased auto traffic. The gatehouse from this period was less than monumental, to say the least. What is of note, however, is what the visitor today sees in its place.

In the late 1980s members of the class of 1943 decided to continue one of the great Academy traditions and fund a memorial. Recognizing the new emphasis of this southern gate (particularly after the Academy purchased Lady Cliff College in 1981), they felt this entrance needed to be more monumental. It needed to signal to the visitor, or new cadet, something of the history, the seriousness, and the architecture of West Point.

This granite building is a compendium of West Point. The vertical massing of the building was derived, in part, from the tower of the Administration Building (#600) (Walk Two). The window on the south was adapted from the fifth-story windows of the 55th Division of the North Barracks. An oriel window on the upper half of the building was inspired by a window formerly above the sallyport of the old North Barracks (now demolished). It features ten blazons in the windows portraying cadet life in the years 1940–43. Corbels supporting the window symbolize the four cadet years with the lower portion, the strongest, the plebe year, supporting the rest. The crenellations are copied from the Ordnance Compound (#637/671 in Walk Five). Adorning the top are finials and fleches copied from the area above the sallyport in the east–west wing of North Barracks.

Many ornamental details cover the exterior of the building. On the south is a two-and-a-half-ton carved limestone USMA crest—carved from a single, four-ton block. The three red-oak doors follow the same shape as the louvered openings of the Cadet Chapel bell tower. The doors' hardware is wrought iron, not cast. The north side, under the window, displays a USMA officer's shield—the graduated cadet will leave the campus as an officer of the United States Army. The neighboring walls that flank the entrance also feature decoration. On the east wall is a bronze plaque with the June 1943 crest. On the west wall, next to the Richard Morris Hunt pillar, is a heraldic crest of the United States. (One can also find a small bronze plaque on the front of the building listing the names of the three main artists who contributed to the building: Doyle (stone carving), Adams (bronze), and City Glass (stained glass).)

The mission to build this small, but robust building required men of equal caliber. They were to be found in the graduates of the class of 1943. Cadets entering the Academy in 1940 found themselves because of the war in an accelerated program, graduating a year earlier than normal. Sixty-two of these men were later killed in battle, more than any other class in Academy history. Survivors who worked on this project contributed concepts and drawings over a number of years in a genuinely collaborative effort. They also raised an extraordinary amount of money, nearly a million dollars, to fund the construction. The Sentry Station and its surroundings provide a unique, useful, and fitting monument to the men of the class of 1943.

3. Thayer Hotel (#674) *Caughy & Evans, 1925*

Hotels at the Academy enjoy a history almost as long as that of the campus itself. Thayer was not the first hotel. As early as 1920 the board of visitors saw the need for suitable accommodation for the Academy's many visitors. The West Point Hotel, situated on the most dramatic eastern point of the Plain, Trophy Point, was built in 1829. With West Point being so far off the beaten track and not yet having rail service, a hotel was an essential part of the Academy's campus. Its modest sixty-four rooms, housed in a Federal style block, were well used by any measure. Few other hotels could boast of such an impressive list of guests: Robert E. Lee, Ulysses S. Grant, Stonewall Jackson, Winfield Scott, William Tecumseh Sherman, Washington Irving, and Edgar Allan Poe and James McNeill Whistler (both of whom were once students at the Academy).

In spite of its legendary visitors, the West Point Hotel did not meet the need of the ever growing school. In 1925 work was begun on a new hotel. The West Point Hotel, after standing empty for many years, was demolished in 1932. Location for the new hotel was to be, perhaps more appropriately, on the southern end of campus, just inside the southern gate. Cram, Goodhue & Ferguson's plan was to place the new hotel at the northern end of campus by the Enlisted Men's Hospital. With the increasing importance placed upon the southern gate, the southern location of the hotel made much more sense. The New York architectural firm Caughy & Evans was hired to design the new larger hotel.

Thayer Hotel, named for Sylvanus Thayer, the Academy's first superintendent, is a five-story building with seven-story towers. It blends in

Thayer Hotel

well with the rest of the Academy's campus in spite of its cheaper brick building material. Aiding the integration are the decorative stone coped parapets and the crenellations of the roofline as well as the dramatic arched granite porte-cochère of the entrance. Atop the capped buttresses are carved stone panels displaying pairs of eagles. Approaching the entrance to the lobby of the Thayer Hotel, one can see one of the original lamps from its older counterpart.

In addition to hosting any visitors to the Academy, the Thayer Hotel also serves the same role of the earlier West Point Hotel: accommodating important visitors. Presidents Eisenhower, Kennedy, Nixon, Ford, and Bush have all stayed here (in the Presidential Suite). Other notable figures include Omar Bradley and Douglas MacArthur, as well as a number of celebrities. Even the fifty-two hostages taken by Iran in 1979 stayed here during their first night back in America.

Thayer Hotel is a handsome addition to the campus; it was included after the competition of 1903, and after the Academy's subsequent expansion, thus placing even more emphasis to the southern end of the school. It is very thoughtfully sited. The hotel rooms on the east side face the river and offer spectacular views down stream. Rooms on the west side are treated to the tidy Buffalo Soldiers Field with its surrounding buildings and the verdant mountain rising behind. From Buffalo Soldiers Field the siting works also; Thayer Hotel completes part of the circle of buildings that neatly ring and embrace the field. One is immediately aware of the encircling of the Cram, Goodhue & Ferguson stables and barracks, and these are complimented by the crenellated elevation of the Thayer Hotel against the backdrop of the Hudson River Valley.

4. Buffalo Soldiers Field Group (#620-628)

Cram, Goodhue & Ferguson (credited to Goodhue), 1903

> A great part of the work at West Point is necessarily of an humbly "practical" character, which does not prevent it from being so picturesque and effective. . . .
>
> —Montgomery Schuyler, architectural critic

The Buffalo Soldiers Field group of buildings is another of the major works contributed to the West Point campus by the winners of the 1903 competition, Cram, Goodhue & Ferguson. Part of the competition guidelines called for designs for barracks and stables. (A riding hall was also mandated and became a central element in the Cram, Goodhue & Ferguson design: Thayer Hall, #601 in Walk Two.) Equestrian skills were still a fundamental part of cadet education until as late as 1947.

Buffalo Soldiers Field Group

The individual buildings are of two designs: the buildings closest to the field are rectangular in plan and plainer in detail and served as stables; those behind have a more varied facade and plan and functioned as barracks. The buildings farther back from the field (#620 and #624) have been greatly modified. Their facades, like those of Buildings #622 and #626, remain intact.

Building #622, formerly the Artillery Stables, serves now as the Enlisted Men's Service Club and Post Library. After a 1914 fire, which destroyed part of the south wing, it was rebuilt in the same style. In 1920 the rear wing was added, and this was converted to a bowling alley in 1959. The former Cavalry Stables (#626) now contains various offices, including housing and transportation. This building has seen a larger number of changes than its counterpart. In 1954 it was converted for use as a warehouse, in 1955 chimneys were removed and a new roof was added, and in 1973 the interior was completely renovated with a new structural system incorporating a second floor. Both buildings share similar facade features: short towers at the terminating ends and a regular articulation created by windows separated with brick pilasters. The portals of the two are not the same. Whereas #626 presents a suitable if less than enthusiastic entrance portal, #622 displays a massive, two-story sallyport set in a tower replete with limestone stringcourses, which accentuate the horizontality of the building, and crenellated parapets, which blend in with the rest of Cram, Goodhue & Ferguson's work for the Academy.

Company Headquarters and Barracks (#620) was designed as barracks for the artillery. As early as 1919 Captain Arthur B. Proctor decided the

Detail Buffalo Soldiers Field Group

building needed expanding and the decision was made to add north and south wings. Again in 1958 and in 1974 other major additions changed the plan. A similar fate was in store for building #624, the former Cavalry Barracks (currently still used for housing). Fortunately for both buildings the structural changes were limited to the back portions; both facades remain nearly intact. The rising central towers correspond to each barracks respective stables situated below and also notify the viewer that these are more than the typically bland dorm type of housing. Visually the exterior is tied together with stringcourses of limestone, connecting the long horizontal facade with the sides. The first floor arcade adds a play of light and shadow echoing the articulation of the stable facades and adding to the comfort and friendliness of the building.

Two more buildings in this area deserve mention as they contributed to the original plan. Building #618 stood where #616 now stands on the south end of the field. Building #616 was designed to be a field artillery gun shed but wound up as the Academy's Visitor Center and, as one can imagine, did not serve its new function with much success. The building fell into such disrepair that in 1987 it was destroyed. Fortunately the administration demanded that any new building placed on this site would have to blend well with the older Cram, Goodhue & Ferguson works. The new Provost Marshall's Office does so admirably, albeit with less aplomb than the older buildings. A different fate was in store for the old Branch Exchange #628, now the Soldiers Club, on the north end of the field. This was the last of the Cram, Goodhue & Ferguson buildings on this part of campus. It still stands but it has been so drastically altered that it is unrecognizable from its original form. (Most of the dramatic changes were in the form of porch additions that extended the front.)

Cram, Goodhue & Ferguson's plan for the buildings was well conceived, excepting their initial desire to locate the group on the north end of the campus. While the administrators had their way with siting the group on this southern end, it was the placement of the various buildings that creates such a notable space. Surrounding the very large Buffalo Soldiers Field and situated in front of the sharply rising mountains, lesser buildings would have been dwarfed by the expanse. Cram, Goodhue & Ferguson placed the buildings in a gently curving arc, surrounding the field, embracing the field, but neither dominating nor overwhelming the setting. Today, thanks to continued thoughtful planning, the group is still highly visible. Nothing has been added, or subtracted, that would disturb the fine view. Although the traditions of teaching cadets horsemanship are long past, this group of undisturbed buildings and the field they surround still remind us of the generations of cadets who daily heard the thundering of hooves.

5.   Officers' Quarters (#21, 25, 32, 34, 42, 45, 48)
Cram, Goodhue & Ferguson, 1908

Just up Thayer Road from the Buffalo Soldiers Field begin some of the Academy's Officers' Quarters. Seven of the houses in this area (four on Thayer and three more on Wilson Road) were part of Cram, Goodhue & Ferguson's continuing relationship with the Academy. These seven houses represent the finest accommodation on the campus, with the possible exception being Cram, Goodhue & Ferguson's similar houses north of the Academic Area on Washington Road (#116, 118, 120, 122). The simplest and best way to see these and the other notable houses on Thayer Road is by walking. There is a well-planned sidewalk on the river side of the street that enables the pedestrian to enjoy views of both the charming homes and the inspiring river valley. (Note: one may drive up Thayer Road for a quick look at the houses, but there is no parking anywhere on this portion of the street.)

These homes were originally designated for captains and lieutenants, and they remain quarters for officers and their families. Although no two of the houses are exactly alike, and some are quite different, they all share some common traits. They are all multiple family structures. Some are for two and some for three families. This sort of economizing aided the ever growing Academy campus by allowing more space for other housing needs and enabling the houses that were built to be quite nice, to say the least.

Number 21 is more distinctively shaped then the rest. It is a three-family house, with two of the units being identical and the third being cross-shaped and extending to the rear. The other houses, duplexes, resemble each other more. These display a variety of shallow projections on the exteriors, enlivening the buildings and adding something of the unpredictability of the Gothic style to the structures. Fenestration on the houses is varied and made more dramatic by two-story window bays. Exterior enrichments, such as the limestone sills and "buttress" caps and the bluestone trim on the chimneys and parapets, lend a greater refinement to the mundane brick. These details really do make the difference on these houses not only in presenting a warm and interesting appearance, as a good home should, but in complementing the Gothic touches found throughout the campus.

Interiors for the houses are also similar: parlor, dining, library, and kitchen on the first floor, bedrooms (often four) and two baths on the second floor, one or two bedrooms, bath, and storerooms on the third floor. (The third floors were usually quarters for household staff and were accessible via a rear staircase only. The main staircase only accesses the first and second floors, surely a maddening situation for modern residents.) What is of exceptional note in these houses are the dramatic Arts and Crafts interiors. All the units have oak and pine floors as well as a variety of wall and ceiling finishes. Wainscotting abounds, at different heights, and many rooms are rich with thickly molded cornices. Some of the homes have cozy window seats. Still evident in a few of the houses are original radiator covers. Clearly the centerpiece of the interiors are the six-foot oak fireplace mantels, each house receiving a different version.

As is evident from much of the rest of Cram, Goodhue & Ferguson's work at the Academy, siting here also plays a key role. Rather than just place the houses at street level, the architects thoughtfully set them back from the road, a main thoroughfare to the Academic Area, and raised them fifteen or so feet above the street level. This arrangement keeps the houses from seeming too "public," and it allows them to take full advantage of the dramatic view of the Hudson Valley; the stone facade of the terraces blends well with other Academy stone work. These houses remain a success as they neatly integrate with the stylistic theme of the rest of the campus and yet remain inviting and intimate homes.

6. Family Housing for Colonel (#5-19)

J. B. Bellinger (based on standardized Office of the Quartermaster plans), 1901

This group of Officers' Quarters stretches from the end of the lower Cram, Goodhue & Ferguson houses on Wilson Road all the way up to the later Cram & Goodhue housing block on Thayer Road, adjacent to the Academic

Area. It forms one of the older housing groups on the campus and represents a distinct period in the architectural history of the Academy.

These houses were constructed shortly before the major 1903 competition and the Academy's massive expansion. Prior to the competition, there was little at this end of the campus. (Even Lady Cliff College did not get started until 1899.) The construction of this housing was clearly an attempt to expand the Academy's campus in a new direction. Its design also reflected, perhaps, admiration for the older Professors' Row, north of the Academic Area. And as with most of the Academy's campus planning, the appeal of the scenic view played a part. Unlike some of the mistakes of their late twentieth-century counterparts, these earlier planners sought to gain spectacular views of the Hudson but not at the expense of blocking others' views.

While houses #5–10 vary stylistically (#8, for example, is a modest brick Queen Anne), houses #11–19 are identical. The latter group displays some of the eclecticism of fin-de-siècle architecture. During the end of the nineteenth century, the Academy had extant Thayer's very Tudor Old Library, Hunt's Romanesque gymnasium and academic building, a mansard roofed administration building, the venerable Doric old Cadet Chapel (now the Cemetery Chapel), and McKim, Mead & White's new Ionic Cullum Hall. Paired columns present on the porches of the five identical houses lend

Family Housing for Colonel

Family Housing for Colonel, Queen Anne style

them a colonial flavor, but the third-level arched window openings and the brackets under the gable returns seem more late nineteenth century.

Much like the Cram, Goodhue & Ferguson houses of a few years later, these homes are also nicely appointed. The houses feature heart pine flooring, and fireplaces are in nearly all the rooms, with the more significant ones receiving elaborate mantels.

While perhaps not as successful and certainly not as expensive as Cram, Goodhue & Ferguson's later houses, this group of homes nonetheless captures a kind of simple elegance. The modest vernacular brick massing, the unpretentious exterior details, the warm wood interiors, and the thoughtful siting all in turn create livable, inviting, and suitable homes for the Academy's officers.

7. Family Housing for Company Grade and Warrant Officer (#1–4) *Cram & Goodhue, 1929*

Originally built as Officers' Quarters, this building was partly converted for nurses' housing in 1935 and now serves as family housing for certain officers. The terraced-style grouping is something unusual for the Academy. With the obvious exception of the barracks, the Academy has no other attached single-building accommodation. Clearly less inspiring than Cram, Goodhue & Ferguson's other houses farther down Thayer Road, it nonetheless succeeds as suitable campus housing.

With a smaller footprint, this building managed to fit against the Academic Area. It also managed to be a more economical approach to housing. Unlike most of their other Academy projects, Cram & Goodhue used steel in the construction, a cost-saving measure. But the building, three stories high in the center, is far from plain. The end bays rise to four stories with the stylized towers. There are cast stone arches above each entrance and a porte-cochère on the east end of the building. Perhaps the most charming detail are the iron railings located on the second and third levels, accessed by functioning French doors.

The building also fits stylistically with the neighboring Academic Area. Although of less expensive brick, which clearly denotes its secondary status, the building is composed of varied square or rectangular masses, lending it a sturdy and fortress-like appearance. Contributing to this effect are the crenellations on portions of the roof and the freestone wall running the length of the building and separating it from the street.

The real story with this building, however, is how it ever was built by Cram & Goodhue in the first place. (By this time, Ferguson had left the firm.) This building was clearly not a part of the 1903 competition—which, although it garnered a reputation for the firm, ended badly. Due to what

Family housing for company grade and warrant officer

must have been a gross bureaucratic mistake, there was a $20,000 error in the billing. Cram's firm thought it the correct pay; the Comptroller of the Treasury thought it an overpayment and refused to make further payments. The firm assured the military that any change in their contract would force them to stop work all together.

This situation grew so grim that in 1918 the Secretary of War nearly involved the Judge Advocate General's office in bringing suit against the firm. By 1927 the issue was resolved, although it is unclear as to how. In any case, letters were again being exchanged and by September of that year Cram himself was writing to the Academy: "Let me assure you that any feeling of gratification you may have at our return to West Point is slight as compared with our feelings in the matter."

Cram & Goodhue could hardly have known this was to be their last building at West Point. (Their entry in the 1944 competition was unsuccessful.) Unfortunately, this situation—and this building—represent a rather mediocre end for the firm that essentially shaped the modern campus.

8. Cadet Activity Club (#696) *A. E. Dougherty, 1924*

Although off the beaten path of the rest of the campus, this small gem of a building is worth the trip. (The visitor will want to drive down to this lower portion of the campus anyway to have a look at the dramatic Academic Area buildings from the river side.) As will be obvious, this building was not originally built as an activity club but as a train station. Not so many years ago, the most utilized method of transport to West Point was rail. New York Central Railroad leased and operated the tracks through West Point until the late 1950s—at which point it was clear rail was out and autos were in. (And *through* West Point is an appropriate term; the careful visitor will want to note that from the station northward the tracks pass under the Academic Area of the campus—yet another sensitive effort to keep the view of the river from the Plain clear of unsightly obstructions.)

The previous station was, like many other parts of the Academy, outgrown. It was built in a Victorian stick style that would not have sat well with the fresh Gothic elements of the 1903 campus. This new station, designed in a manner of Gothic not quite in keeping with the rest of the campus, is much more elaborate and very nearly too precious. What prevents the building from being gauche is its wholehearted attempt at being something grand.

With the exception of the extended canopy, the exterior of the building remains true to its design. The light colored brick is similar to some of the Academic Area buildings but, as with the style of the building itself, is mostly singular. There are a plethora of exterior enrichments: the limestone sills and quoins, the crenellations, and the stylized buttresses and towers.

Cadet Activity Club

The visitor will especially want to note the charming octagonal chimney on the northwest side of the building. All of this is, of course, too much for a building this small, except that it works in exactly the way planned for the function of this building.

So too with the wonderfully lavish interior. Inside, the building once contained a waiting room, a smoking room, men's and ladies' toilets, a baggage room, and a ticket office. The north end of the interior has been mostly modified for current use, but the southern end, the waiting room, is original. Peeking through the leaded-glass windows reveals a warm and inviting room of wood. Tongue and groove chamfered oak wainscotting covers the lower walls, plaster the upper, and dramatic pine planks are exposed on the open rafter ceiling. There are four exposed trusses that feature acorn pendants. An oak bench runs along the sides of the room, and opposite the heavy entrance doors is a large and inviting fireplace.

The new station attempts to echo the vastness of its big-city counterparts. The high ceilings and rich materials refer, on a less costly scale, to the vast spaces of Union and Grand Central. But for what purpose could all this have possibly have been? Before the days of the prolific car ownership, new cadets often traveled via rail to begin their lives at the Academy. After hours, or perhaps days, of journeying, this small station presented the first impression of the Academy to the cadet. This station would, for just a few moments, introduce the cadet to the stately new surroundings and hint, in a gentle way, of the monumental architectural environment that would be his new home.

Academic Area

9	Mahan Hall
10	Administration Building
11	Sherman Barracks and Lee Barracks
12	Taylor Hall
13	Grant Hall / New South Barracks
14	Pershing Barracks
15	Old Central Barracks
16	Bartlett Hall
17	Thayer Hall
18	Power House
19	Officers' Mess and Quarters
20	Cullum Hall
21	Lincoln Hall
22	USMA Library
23	Washington Hall
24	Scott Barracks
25	Arvin Gymnasium

Grant Hall detail

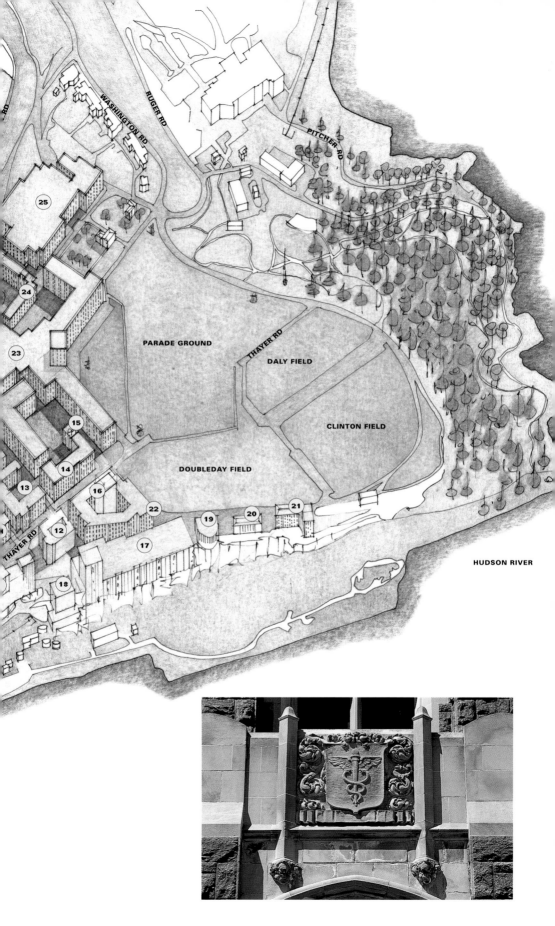

WASHINGTON RD

RUGER RD

PITCHER RD

PARADE GROUND

THAYER RD

DALY FIELD

CLINTON FIELD

DOUBLEDAY FIELD

THAYER RD

HUDSON RIVER

25

24

23

15

14

13

16

12

17

18

22

19

20

21

Stone and Plain

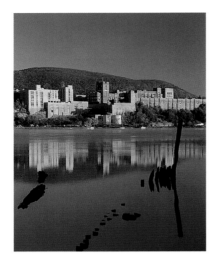

Early morning along the Hudson River

The Academic Area is, and always has been, the heart of the United States Military Academy. From its earliest conception as an institution, two things have remained almost entirely consistent: the arrangement of the buildings around the Plain and the use of the Plain. The Academy's founders thought that the best use of the area known as West Point was one that placed the buildings in an encircling plan about the Plain while attempting to keep the eastern, river side of the campus unobstructed. With only a few exceptions, this has remained the case at the Academy. The buildings of the Academic Area create an embrace of the Plain; the places cadets go to exercise their minds surround the place where cadets go to exercise their bodies.

None of this means that the early founders of the Academy had the slightest idea that the Academic Area would some day be as it is now. The scale of the modern buildings was of course inconceivable back then—and only became possible with the advent of the revolutionary steel I-beam. Early buildings on the Plain were of a much more modest nature. Period drawings show simple, rectangular buildings, often brick. As with many early American colleges, these buildings served multiple purposes: classrooms, barracks, offices, storage. Like the buildings back then, life at the Point was much simpler. Slowly the Academic Area developed, a few buildings here, a few there. The first major growth came about under the able leadership of Major Richard Delafield in 1838.

Trained in military fortification Delafield was clearly the right man at the right time. A fire in one of the academic buildings just prior to his arrival put his talents to the test. Delafield's influence was key in at least three major works, the Old Library, old Central Barracks, and the Ordnance Compound. His real contribution lay in more than just the buildings themselves, it was his attempt at establishing a coherent architectural style for the campus. Most agree that he succeeded admirably, although it isn't terribly clear as to what style he promoted. What he wanted was not precisely what was built, particularly in the Central Barracks. Part Tudor, part Gothic, and part Norman, it no doubt influenced later builders.

The next significant period of building came about right at the end of the century. In 1889 Congress appropriated the funds for a new gym and a new academic building for the United States Military Academy. The architect selected for the job was Richard Morris Hunt. A more suitable architect could hardly have been found. Hunt, the first American to be trained at the École des Beaux-Arts. After his education he was the first American to open an atelier in New York in order to train young architects in the Beaux-Arts style, of which he was a profound adherent. Hunt's efforts helped to launch the Beaux-Arts style in America. He was the most influential architect of his generation. At the Academy, Hunt's work contributed a hearty vigor. It was rugged and masculine with towers and crenellations and suited the campus well.

Following right after Hunt's work was that of the well-known firm, McKim, Mead & White. This firm enjoyed a very successful career; practicing in the Beaux-Arts style they produced more than 500 buildings. Among their most well known works are the Boston Public Library, and in New York the Morgan Library and Penn Station (demolished 1964). Their two West Point buildings, the Officers' Mess and Cullum Hall, were not designed in any variant of Gothic—such as was typically found on the campus at that time—but rather were classical in style. Fortunately the strength of the two buildings, perched side by side on the edge of the Plain, gives them a certain cool dignity. However, classical forms were not what the Academy wanted when it came time for its largest and most famous expansion.

It was evident by the end of the century that one or two new buildings every decade or so would not suffice. In 1899 the Academy's board of visitors recognized that the Academy needed major additions to its physical plant. After two reports from the very able Charles W. Larned, professor of drawing (who had been proclaiming the need for a coherent campus plan for years), the federal government in 1901 approved $5.5 million for the work. Larned's second report was comprehensive and detailed and not only suggested locations for the new buildings but clearly leaned toward a particular style: "It is of the highest importance to preserve intact the structural sentiment which gives character and individuality to the Academy." The style that was begun by Delafield has been called Tudor-Gothic.

A competition was organized in 1902. Invitations were sent out to several firms: Cope & Stewardson, Hines & LaFarge, Carrère & Hastings, Peabody & Stearns, Armes & Young, Charles C. Haight, Daniel H. Burnham, Cram, Goodhue & Ferguson, McKim, Mead & White, and Frost & Grainger. Judging the entries were Superintendent Robert Mills, former Superintendent John M. Schofield, and three architects: George B. Post, Walter Cook, and Cass Gilbert. Despite missing an organizational meeting of the entrants and not being permitted to submit perspective drawings in their proposal (a detriment to Gothic designs) the then little known firm of Cram, Goodhue & Ferguson was selected. The most surprised was perhaps Cram himself—who wasn't exactly sure why the firm had been chosen for the competition in the first place. After receiving congratulations from Larned, Cram replied with this explanation of their plan:

> We made as deep a study of all the conditions as was possible. We immediately saw that the whole problem was primarily one in arrangement; first, from an administrative, second, from a pictorial standpoint. This relation was, however, absolute, the question of administration taking precedence of everything else.

Some were less than pleased by the selection of the rustic Gothic design. Stanford White, whose plan included removing most of the existing buildings and substituting classical ones, thought the selection of Gothic "a body blow to all those who are striving to raise architecture out of the heterogeneous mush." There were other complaints that the jury had known all along that Gothic was the preferred choice. Looking back, it is not hard to recognize that Cram, Goodhue & Ferguson simply followed the plan as laid out by Larned and the Academy and recognized the traditional campus style. Whether this was from immaturity or shrewdness is irrelevant—it won them the commission.

Nearing one hundred years old, the works that Cram, Goodhue & Ferguson designed remain today almost as they were built. Their vision of a rustic, masculine, militaristic Gothic campus is enjoyed by every visitor and cadet. However, there were at least two variants that very nearly came to be and might have seriously altered the campus. The first was the placement of the Chapel. Larned had pushed to have it situated on the edge of the Plain, to be visible on all sides. Cram, writing in his autobiography, states that he selected the present location for the Chapel upon his first visit to the Point. On the other hand, Cram was insistent that a new, large Superintendent's Quarters be constructed on the northeastern edge of the Plain. Fortunately, the board decided against this.

Thus was established the portion of the campus that is so well known. The next notable architect who attempted to design structures sympathetic in style and massing to those of Cram was Paul Philippe Cret. Cret was one of the nation's finest architects in the Beaux-Arts style. Although the Beaux-Arts style favored classicism, Cret skillfully drew from a variety of past styles during a very successful career as architect and teacher. His talents were broad and he designed government buildings (the Pan American Union and the Federal Reserve, both in Washington, D.C.), art museums (the Rodin Museum, Philadelphia, and the Detroit Institute of Fine Arts), memorials (Washington Memorial Arch, Valley Forge), houses, and even complete trains—both engines and interiors (the Zephyr and the Empire State). Scott Barracks and the Bartlett Hall addition, two of Cret's buildings in the Academic Area, both echo the rustic Gothic of Cram, Goodhue & Ferguson's work but remain distinct. Like other later architects at the

Point in the fog

Academy, Cret managed to remain true to the style and complement the campus but also bring a subtle new depth.

And so it went in the Academic Area. After Cret's notable work there were fewer projects but those few were of a scale unprecedented. In 1946 Delano & Aldrich completed the very lavish Gothic Washington Hall; in 1965 O'Connor & Kilham increased the size of Washington with a rustic Gothic addition that doubled its already considerable size. Its facade now defines the Academic Area in such a strong way that it is hard to imagine the space without it. Washington Hall was the last of the major commissions in the Academic Area and this is a good thing. The Academy has worked hard, with great success, at not crowding too much onto the Plain. It has also managed, amazingly, to keep most of the eastern edge of the Plain unobstructed.

The Academic Area remains, as it has for so long, an inspiring and multifaceted place. One is cozy in the nearness of the buildings, but they are made of harsh, rough stone; one marvels at the scale and craft evident in the granite halls but also at the spectacular beauty of the bluff and river. This area does not exhibit the same qualities as a small liberal arts college. The area is intimate but not warm, it embraces but does not coddle. The Academy, perhaps like the military, suggests a particular kind of rapport: fraternity. It embraces not as a mother does a child but as a brother does a brother. The Academy is not alma mater, but rather *alma frater*.

Mahan Hall

9. Mahan Hall (#752) *R. B. O'Connor & W. H. Kilham, 1972*

Architects O'Connor & Kilham, known for their library designs—Princeton's Firestone Library, the Schneider Library at the University of Louisville, and the National Library of Medicine in Bethesda, Maryland—were in the unenviable position of attempting a major new building for one of the most famous architectural groupings on one of the most famous campuses in the world. It was not to their advantage that they were asked to do so during the 1970s. What they designed was a very large building with little detail but with some thought to its placement and massing.

Between 1964 and 1972 the Academy increased its enrollment from 2,529 to 4,417. Such tremendous growth meant more facilities were needed quickly. When the Academy Board looked into constructing something on the scale of Mahan Hall, they were not pleased to find that building costs had increased significantly. Although cost increases slowed plans down, problems in siting created more significant problems. Very steep slopes caused difficulties in creating the concrete foundation for the building. Two years behind schedule, the building finally opened in 1972.

Mahan Hall is massed interestingly, with various sections of between four and six stories and towers on both the north and south wings. Mahan was to straddle Cullum Road in hopes of alleviating traffic around the campus. Certainly, the building was inserted into the fabric of the campus with great forethought. On the river side it appears that the various elevations of the building's parts are set upon a kind of rustic "foundation." This lends the work a rugged appearance and also lends variety to the structure as a whole. It is not a dull building. However, this evaluation holds most true from far away; from across the river, one might be hard pressed to date Mahan Hall. The granite facade blends in well with Thayer Hall next door and continues the fortress-like appearance of the campus.

Up close, however, the building is less impressive. The lack of ornament and even of stone trim brings the structure up short. (To be fair, there is a tiny bit of stone work on the towers, but it is hardly noticeable.) Half-hearted at best, the few crenellations are stylized and do not lend that rhythmic dance to the roofline. Worst of all are the very dated and dreadfully plain windows. They are connected in vertical bands with mechanistic corrugated aluminum spandrels.

Mahan Hall is named for Dennis Hart Mahan, an 1824 graduate of the Academy and professor of engineering at the Academy from 1832–71. A plaque on the exterior of the building marks it as a National Historic Civil Engineering Landmark. The Military Academy, predating both the University of Virginia and Rensselaer Polytechnic Institute, is the oldest extant institute in America to offer formal training in civil engineering. (Teaching in civil engineering began at the Academy in September 1813.)

10. Administration Building (#606)

Arnold W. Brunner, 1920–23; addition, 1932; York & Sawyer, addition, 1942

Although this building has been heavily modified, it still maintains something of its original design. Situated along Thayer Road, architect Arnold Brunner's work started off as a large addition to the 1884 hospital, doubling that building's size. The building was hardly up ten years when the first of many additions began. In 1932 a large wing was added on the west side; in 1942 York & Sawyer added a fourth floor and the westernmost addition.

Administration Building, Lee, Grant, and Pershing Barracks

Administration Building

During the late fifties the interior was heavily modified and by 1959 the final standing wing of the original building was demolished. Keller Hospital was opened in 1977; Leo A. Daly III's work in 1981 included modifications to the interior for use as an administration building. All that remains of Brunner's original work is the Thayer Road facade, the south elevation, and a vaulted vestibule just inside the doors.

Brunner had experience on other institutional buildings, such as his School of Mines at Columbia University, the Students' Building at Barnard College, and the Jewish Hospital in Brooklyn. His work for the

Administration Building, Retreat symbols

Academy demonstrates a willingness to work within the traditions set by the other Thayer Road buildings and a confidence to include suitable variations. The building is granite, as expected, but features leaded glass for the windows, the top story ones nicely arched.

An array of medical symbols was placed above the leaded glass casements of the first floor. (Although these have long been replaced, the visitor may get an idea of the symbols from caduceus above the portal.) Placed along the cornice of the third floor is a multitude of charming grotesques.

The Administration Building is an example of Academy economics leading to the deterioration of a fine building. Clearly, Brunner's work was superior to any of the additions; the fourth floor addition is rather pitiful. Yet Brunner's work is still partly visible, and the visitor may acknowledge the careful design elements that were included at a time when ornament and delight were still essential parts of any good building.

11. Sherman Barracks (#738) and Lee Barracks (#740)

R. B. O'Connor & W. H. Kilham, 1962

Although these two barracks obviously represent later additions to the campus, O'Connor & Kilham nonetheless attempted to keep these buildings within the rustic Gothic campus style. Facing Thayer Road, Lee Barracks has the difficult task of blending in with the earlier neighboring works—not an easy thing during the 1960s when most contextual architecture was frowned upon.

The buildings are five stories above ground, six on the east side. While not huge, they are substantial buildings. Aiding to the strength in Lee is the Thayer Road facade, which features a detail which is decorative but doesn't deserve to be called a buttress but does push the windows back a bit, lending the front a bit of rhythm and articulation. Some of the concrete spandrels feature leaf motifs or a modification of the USMA coat of arms. On the north and on the east (interior), the first story is set back so as to create useful galleries. Perhaps the most effective element is the high granite

Lee Barracks and Sherman Barracks, left to right

wall facing Thayer, with a sprinkling of charming and tiny windows, that helps to distinguish the front of the building and divide it from the road.

None of these details, however, can rescue a building that seems half-hearted at best. Its massing does not fit at all with the rest of the campus; it is hard to believe these buildings were placed within sight of Cram's thoughtfully massed Taylor Hall. Of course, O'Connor & Kilham were attempting to strip the building down to its essential components, a popular pastime with modernist architects. What they created was not a rugged, handsome and timeless rustic Gothic monument but a plain rectangle of a building with tedious fenestration and massing that is frankly boring.

12. Taylor Hall / Administration Building (#600)

Cram, Goodhue & Ferguson (credited to Cram), 1905–10

> When one, in the climb of the hill and at the turn of the road, comes upon the deep and dark arched portal, flanked and abutted by its barbican, which is the chief entrance to the place, he cannot help being impressed with the absolute appropriateness of the cliff-like tower, with its stunted battlements, alike to the purpose and to the place.
>
> —Montgomery Schuyler, architectural critic

Excepting only the Cadet Chapel, no other building on the Academy campus quite symbolizes the school like Taylor Hall. Situated in the heart of the Academy, this solid masonry building strikes exactly the right note. This is

Cullum Road and Thayer, Mahan, Taylor, and Bartlett Halls

not a building to reflect utilitarian values. It is a building which architect Ralph Adams Cram imbued with symbolism and enriched with a myriad of ornament, suitable enough for the main administration building of an ever growing military academy.

  The exterior features the same rustic granite and limestone as the other Cram, Goodhue & Ferguson buildings. What is unique is the attention to detail for every aspect of the building. The southeast corner, itself treated like a tower, was to have provided offices for the superintendent and other administrators. The superintendent's office is designated by the balcony on the second story of the

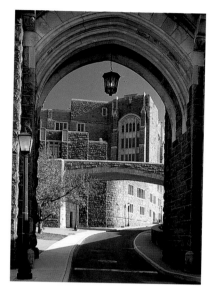

Taylor Hall and Bartlett Hall beyond

east side. A large, arched window on the lower level identifies a space used for the adjutant general's courtroom.

  Rising 160 feet above Cullum Road, the tower reaches an impressive height for a masonry edifice. Local lore claims it is the tallest all-stone masonry building in the world. (Philadelphia City Hall, in fact, at more than 500 feet tall, is the tallest and largest masonry building in the world.) The tower contains more office space. Attached to the bottom of the tower is a curious porte-cochère with a squat turret. Because of the construction of Mahan Hall in 1972, and the related raising up of Cullum Road, something

Taylor Hall Porte-cochère

Taylor Hall detail

Taylor Hall, sallyport to courtyard

of the placement of not only the porte-cochère but the entire building has been lost. Before the later additions Taylor acted as a gateway to the Academic Area, standing as a dramatic fortress, leading the visitor—by the more humanly scaled and curious porte-cochère—toward the "summit."

On the north side of the building the upper two levels feature delicate traceried windows. These indicate the Academic Board Room, the Faculty Lounge, and Lee Hall, originally part of the Ordnance Museum, three of the more notable interior areas of the building. It is the west facade, however, where we find the monumental sallyport that signifies the main entrance to the building.

Facing this entrance, the visitor will note some of the many crests located around the building. These are heraldic shields of the fifty states and territories. (For example, on the bottom of the right row is the crest for Arkansas.) The two larger shields at the top of these rows represent the War Department and the Corps of Engineers. At the very top of the facade is an unfinished eagle sculpture. Due to some cost overruns, the quartermaster's office ran out of money and could no longer pay the sculptor, Lee Lawrie. Years later, when funds became available, Lawrie came to inspect the work only to find that it had been softly weathered in the elements. He refused to continue the work, thinking what nature had done was better than what he could achieve.

(The sallyport and courtyard are open to the public.) Moving through the sallyport, one finds shields representing the multiple staff departments of a headquarters: adjutant generals, quartermasters, ordnance department, and so forth. Passing through the sallyport leads one under the massive (fake) portcullis into the courtyard. Here are located more state shields, George Washington's coat of arms, and certain names carved in stone: Williams (Colonel Jonathan Williams, first superintendent of the Academy), Swift (Colonel Joseph G. Swift, first graduate), Totten (General Joseph G. Totten, ex-officio the first inspector of the Academy), Thayer (Colonel Sylvanus Thayer, Father of the Academy), Delafield

Taylor Hall Academic Board Room

(Colonel Richard Delafield, superintendent from 1856 to 1861, under whose administration much construction was completed), Jefferson (Thomas Jefferson, third president of the United States, under whose administration the Academy was founded), and Monroe (James Monroe, fifth president of the United States, under whose administration the Academy developed and flourished).

The interior of the building, as one would expect, also features a variety of rich details. The main stair hall has quarry tiled floors, vaulted ceilings, and brick walls with limestone trim. Lee Hall, restored in the 1970s, has slate floors, a vaulted ceiling with limestone trim, and leaded glass windows. In the faculty lounge one can find barrel vaults made with Guastavino

Taylor Hall Academic Board Room; fire-place by Lee Lawrie

tiles and terracotta ribs. The Super-intendent's Office features rich oak paneling, molded plaster ceilings, a dramatic carved fireplace, and photo-graphs of all past superintendents.

The crowning achievement of the interior spaces may be found in the Academic Board Room. In addition to the oak wainscotting and the leaded windows is a monumental stone fire-place carved by Lee Lawrie. Contained in the mantel are nine figures, some mythic, from military history: Joshua, Hector, David, Alexander the Great, Julius Caesar, Charlemagne, King Arthur, Godfrey de Bouillon, and Judas Maccabeus. Each of these has a small shield underneath with some defining attribute for identification.

(For example, under the figure of King Arthur is a shield bearing the Holy Grail.) The figures are arranged chronologically and historically, three hea-then, three Christian, three Jewish. Architect Cram came up with this group-ing after reading William Caxton's preface to Thomas Malory's *Morte d'Arthur*. The mantel is a stunning symbol and reminder for the leadership of the Academy who gather in this room.

13. Grant Hall / New South Barracks (#602)

Gehron & Ross, 1930

Grant Hall, built after the major projects of 1903, reflects many of the posi-tive qualities of later additions to the campus. Considering the building's location on Thayer Road, this was critical to its integration. On its north side is Hunt's rugged Pershing Barracks (#751), and directly across Thayer Road are Cram, Goodhue & Ferguson's Bartlett Hall and Taylor Hall. To the south was Brunner's refined hospital building (which has since been heavily modi-fied). Fortunately, Gehron & Ross were up to the task and designed a build-ing that suitably fits with the other stern granite faces along Thayer Road.

When standing in front of Grant Hall, the viewer is actually seeing only a small part of the entire structure. Grant Hall is the first floor portion of the building that extends toward Thayer Road. It was built on the site of the old Grant Hall, the original cadet's mess. Distinguishing it from the rest of the building is its projection and different fenestration. New South

Grant Hall/New South Barracks

Barracks is the rest of the building, most of which is only partly visible from the road. There is no connecting passage between the two.

Gehron & Ross conceived of a C-shaped building that added something of a new element to the campus. Although the Academy has certain spaces formed between buildings (the most famous being The Walk behind Pershing Barracks (#751)), no one had yet built a "quad." Not only does Gehron & Ross' design create a more intimate space, something not undesirable for quarters, it provides an opportunity to economize; the inside of the quad, mostly concealed, is constructed of cheaper brick.

Grant Hall detail

The facade of the building maintains the more elaborate granite treatment, sheathing in this case, with the added benefit of a few limestone details. Cadets holding rifles flank the main entrance. Above is carved "Grant Hall" in Art Deco–style lettering.

Grant Hall details

Grant Hall, interior painted beams

The Academy annual report of 1932 states: "The first floor of this building contains the Cadet Reception room, well designed and furnished with taste. It fills a real need for a place where parents and friends of the cadets can visit the cadets during release from quarters. The Cadet Hostess has an office at the north end of the reception room where she is readily accessible to the cadets and their friends." The hostess is no longer present, but any visitor to the campus will want to step inside of Grant Hall. (You are more than welcome to sit and enjoy the room but unaccompanied visitors wishing to dine must bring their own food.)

Greeting the visitor is a lavish room with the intimacy of a New York City men's club. Exposed beams and joists cover the ceiling. (They are cleverly painted concrete and not wood.) Adorning the beams are painted seals of the states and insignia from the military divisions of World War I as well as a myriad of decorative details. Arched limestone portals lead to more intimate dining spaces. A majestic paneled fireplace crowns one end. Portraits of five star generals are hung about the room. The furnishings are inviting, too, with thickly padded chairs, dark wooden tables, and cozy patterned rugs. Visitors will find themselves lingering.

14. Pershing Barracks (#751)

Richard Morris Hunt, 1891–1895; Gehron & Seltzer, renovation, 1956

Although most well known for two Vanderbilt family homes, Biltmore in Asheville, North Carolina, and The Breakers in Newport, Rhode Island, Hunt also designed many other buildings. Among his other works were many office buildings in New York (most of which have been destroyed), the original Fogg Art Museum at Harvard (renamed Hunt Hall after the architect), the base for the Statue of Liberty, the Administration Building for the very influential 1893 World's Columbian Exposition, and the first construction for the

Metropolitan Museum of Art. Perhaps more to the point, just prior to his engagement for the Academy, Hunt drew up plans for the United State Naval Observatory in Washington. It appeared that Hunt was the perfect choice for the Academy.

But things did not go smoothly for either Hunt or the Academy. Although Congress had appropriated $490,000 for the academic building, with twelve percent going to Hunt's fee and miscellaneous costs only $431,000 remained for the building.

Similar problems faced the gymnasium, Hunt's other big project at the Academy. Hunt's plans for the gym were drawn up in three months, but when given to the contractors projections ran about $19,000 over what they had to spend. To make matters worse, Superintendent Wilson, who had been reminding Hunt all along to keep costs down, found Hunt's estimate to contain about $7,000 in mathematical errors, thus pushing the estimates that much higher. A later error was discov-

Exterior of Gymnasium, Richard Morris Hunt, c. 1891. Demolished 1924.

ered when Hunt submitted final working drawings; the building was one foot shorter than on the specifications. The Academy Board was not pleased and was hesitant about letting Hunt continue with the building. Things got worse: there were problems with the superintendent of works (who was fired) and problems with the contractor (who quit).

Pershing Barracks

Pershing Barracks, sallyport

Hunt's plans for the academic building were rife with problems also. At first his plans were much too grand and would have been over budget. The Academy had very specific requirements for the new building which they suggested Hunt follow. Professor Charles W. Larned, so influential in much of the subsequent architecture at the Academy, thought Hunt's attitude toward the projects less than suitable. Eventually the plans were settled and building commenced; after problems with the roof design, the building was finished in 1895, about two years behind schedule.

Pershing Barracks

Inside, the academic building has been utterly changed from the original. Many of the original drawings are missing or damaged and it is difficult to piece together just exactly what the interior looked like. There were a variety of classrooms and labs, some with dramatic two-story ceilings. Skylights were used to illuminate stairwells and the fourth floor. In 1956 Gehron & Seltzer were selected to renovate the interior and did so completely. The building was renamed Pershing Barracks and is still used for cadet housing.

Outside little has changed. Hunt selected a Massachusetts granite for the exterior. The ashlar granite is more rusticated, and rugged, than that found on other Academy buildings. Lighter in color too, the granite is used throughout creating a very uniform structure. Clearly taking a cue from the earlier Delafield buildings (especially the Ordnance Compound), Hunt also worked in a kind of Tudor style. The building is symmetrical, reflecting something of Hunt's Beaux-Arts taste, but it is not classical nor does it have classical elements. A sallyport divides the east facade; leading upward from the sallyport are two vertical bands terminating in thin crenellated towers with pointy drain spouts. On the north-east corner a square tower, replete with gargoyles, breaks the symmetry but lends the building some needed height. The tower is crenellated with the same regularity as is the roof. Further breaking up the symmetry is a fourth floor balcony on the south end of the building. Enriching the entire building is the band of stone brackets just under the parapet. These brackets offer a dramatic repetition of light and

Pershing Barracks

Pershing Barracks gargoyle

shadow that makes the building seem more delicate than it is.

The siting of Hunt's building has played an important role in the significance of this work. Its location lends to the drama of the Thayer Road group, but it was also clearly visible from the Plain. (It is less visible today, blocked partially by Washington Hall.) The building's C-shape also created an important space behind the building, perhaps the best known to cadets at the Academy: the "area." Few are the cadets who have not been required to "walk the area."

Hunt's academic building continued and affirmed the tradition of trying to find a suitable style for the Academy as a whole. His work tried, and succeeded, in fitting with the newer Delafield buildings. No doubt his work later influenced Cram, Goodhue & Ferguson in their stylistic choices. Indeed, when Hunt's academic building was completed, it was one of the largest buildings on campus, foreshadowing the even larger projects of just a few years later.

Old Central Barracks

15. Old Central Barracks (#747)

Richard Delafield, circa 1839–1845

Little is left today of the Old Central Barracks. Only one tiny end tower section, kept because of the strength of tradition, is all that remains. This one section is thick with history, as was the whole building. Not only did Old Central Barracks house some of the Academy's most distinguished cadets, it initiated both the housing tradition and the architectural style of the Academy.

Major Richard Delafield became superintendent of the Academy in 1838. He had been in the first class examined by Sylvanus Thayer and was much the disciple of Thayer's method. He came to the Academy with a sedulous frame of mind and immediately set to work. Delafield's work included tightening up cadet discipline, streamlining cadet responsibilities, and supervising schedules and architecture. A fire earlier in 1838 destroyed much of the 1815 Academy building. The previous superintendent, Rene E.

DeRussy, had begun working toward some new replacement buildings. Delafield picked up where DeRussy left off but became more personally involved. Along with three faculty members, Delafield attempted to work up some kind of a campus plan. To aid them in this endeavor was Isaiah Rogers, a New York architect well known for his Greek Revival work. Delafield was not impressed with Rogers' plans; he did not think a classical style suitable for the Academy.

Frederick Diaper, an architect born and trained in England, was recruited. Diaper may have come to recognition for an Italianate home he built for William Paterson van Rensselaer of Albany, "Beverwyck." For Delafield's perusal, Diaper submitted drawings in more of a Gothic style. Delafield liked Diaper's work and commented upon the style at length:

> It embraces all that is judged necessary, without any superfluities, to the eye, but suited to the surrounding scenery and in accordance with collegiate buildings elsewhere. Another design after this style of architecture has presented itself to my mind, better adapted to the locality when considered in connection with the adjacent buildings.

In what would be a monumental move for the Academy, Delafield submitted his own drawings, borrowing heavily from Diaper, in something of a Tudor-Gothic style. Delafield's barracks were built, as well as the Old Library and the Ordnance Compound, all in this odd amalgam blend that would become the Academy's trademark style.

Delafield's design featured a strong rectangular, symmetrical building with a dramatic central entrance complete with a two-story oriel window and small crenellated towers and flanking towers on either end, each with its own onion-dome. (Observation instruments were at one time installed in the domes but were later removed due to disturbance of the train. The domes were eventually removed, too.) The granite masonry of the building carried the weight and was embellished with red sandstone trim on the turrets, above the windows, and the stringcourse.

Delafield's plan for the barracks was simple: the four-story building was divided into divisions, each having four rooms per floor, two rooms on each side of a stair hall, with no communication between divisions. (Barracks have remained this way.) Old Central Barracks was designed to be fireproof, with firewalls separating each division. Along the back of the building ran a very useful and used porch. Although the building was to be used primarily as a barracks, the original plans designated some rooms for other purposes: one for the department of history, geography, ethics, two for dentists, two for bath rooms, nine for storehouses and armories, and five for "Light Prisons for Cadets."

Today it is the interior of what is left of the Old Central Barracks that will be of interest to the visitor. Unfortunately Old Central Barracks is

Old Central Barracks, Pershing's room

off-limits to unescorted guests. Those lucky enough to gain entrance will find a few rooms with their original period furnishings from the section that housed the First Division. These cadet rooms are even more spartan than those of today but did have the luxury of a fireplace. (No one is quite sure if these functioned, as the building was known to have been heated with steam. Period photos show them decorated or holding items, not filled with coal.) A few of the rooms are still equipped with the original wooden partitions that separated the two cadet beds. Most notable is the second floor tower room. Traditionally, tower rooms were held by the highest ranking cadets. This particular room was home to both John J. Pershing, class of 1886, and Douglas MacArthur, class of 1903, when each was First Captain. George Patton was also housed in Old Central Barracks, but not in a tower room.

The entire scope of the building with its various wings and renovations took nearly seventy years to complete. By the early 1960s, however, it was clear that the building was obsolete and in 1969 it was set for demolition. Fortunately, by the late 1960s the preservation movement growing and a portion of the building was saved. Clearly, Old Central Barracks was in rough shape and the decision to preserve this small but significant corner was a good compromise. One can hardly imagine the campus without this part of Academy history.

16. Bartlett Hall (#753)

Cram, Goodhue & Ferguson, 1903–13; Paul Cret, addition, 1938; addition, 1953

Surely there are few other buildings in America with such a pedigree. Bartlett Hall is actually two buildings and, when viewed from the exterior, might be thought to include a third building, the library. The first section of the building was originally called simply the East Academic Building. This portion, essentially a rectangle, faces Thayer Road and was part of the Cram, Goodhue & Ferguson competition work. It was perpendicular to the Old Library (which stood on the site of the new library). In 1938 Cret's work doubled the size of the structure by adding a wing behind the East Academic Building. Cret's building runs diagonally from the south end of Cram, Goodhue & Ferguson's building to the east end of the Old Library. (It was actually connected to Cram, Goodhue & Ferguson's building.) By 1953 more space was required for the library and the Moore wing was added; by 1963 the Old Library was demolished, the new library built in its place, and all three buildings connected to form the triangular structure as it is today.

Cram, Goodhue & Ferguson's original building was simple in shape but with the refinement of detail that one would expect. Viewing the building from Thayer Road, the visitor will notice that the building is presented in three parts. Each part contains its own portal, the center section receiving a sculpted version of the USMA shield above the doorway. On either side of the center section of the building are "towers." The "towers," not much more than a few extra feet high and protruding forward slightly, act as a

Bartlett Hall, Cram wing

Bartlett Hall, Cram wing, details

visual terminus; they break up what would otherwise be a very long building and move the eye upward. Slight buttresses on the facade also lead the eye up as well as articulate the windows. The latter are highlighted by the use of much lighter stone, which contrasts well with the local, dark granite. Finally, the fenestration of the building, while very regular in the center, is not in the ends (although they are symmetrical). The building is long and low, rhythmic and regular but the sensitive details keep it from being heavy and staid.

Boyd Wheeler Bartlett, for whom the building was named, was first in his class (1826) and went on to be named acting professor of natural and experimental philosophy, a post he held for 37 years. Bartlett was one of the original members of the National Academy of Sciences and one of the first scientists to use photography for astronomy. The Old Library contained a workshop and observatory he created with some of the best instruments of his day. Naturally, the hall named after him, the first twentieth-century classroom building at the Academy, would follow in kind. When built Bartlett Hall contained a variety of skylights as well as an observation gallery with telescope dome. Cret's addition to the building continued the support of the growing scientific classroom needs of the Academy. It was designed to contain a variety of very specific research spaces. These included a natural and experimental philosophy lab, a new electrical lab, sections rooms, instructors' rooms, offices, and a library.

Cret's 1938 addition, one of several projects he worked on during the 1930s, is best seen from Cullum Road. The solution Cret came up with for placing the building alongside the road is subtle and very successful. He did not have to block valuable road space, he was able to connect his work to the original building, and he did not take up more space than necessary. What makes all of this even more compelling is that he was able to design a building that fits in with neighboring buildings but also stands out as work by another hand. Cret managed to create a different look by using large stone window trim connecting the top three floors. The contrasting, recessed stone gives the effect of long, Gothic windows in the perpendicular style, when the windows are in fact simple and basic rectangles. The lower windows have mullions that lend an appearance of leaded windows. Subtle stone buttresses and crenellation complete the look of a true military academy building.

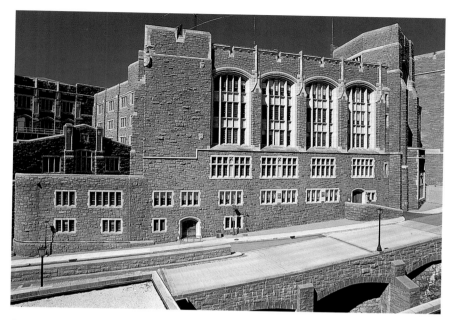

Bartlett Hall, Cret addition

The exteriors of the two buildings have been modified, but not too badly. Cram, Goodhue & Ferguson's building has been greatly modified to the rear (east) side with many additions. (While it was never constructed, the reader might be interested in knowing that Larned, it appears, had hoped for a massive connecting "screen" running from Bartlett to Hunt's Pershing Barracks across Thayer Road. This Gothic "Memorial Bridge" would have been as tall as the buildings to which it was connected. It was to feature various sculptures of notable alumni and to act as a kind of monumental gateway to the heart of the campus.) The interior of Cret's building has remained mostly unchanged, but Cram, Goodhue & Ferguson's has been utterly altered, much to the detriment of the building. In 1960 Louis Gardner was hired to "renovate" the interior of the building. This included removal of most of the original wood wainscot, doors, and transoms as well as arches and stone piers, columns, partitions, and handrails. The skylights were covered. The ceilings were dropped, presumably for duct work, and new partitions and radiators added. Most depressingly the wooden parquet floor was covered over with vinyl-asbestos tiles. Fortunately the visitor is not allowed inside.

View downriver past Thayer Hall

17. Thayer Hall (#601)

Cram, Goodhue & Ferguson (credited to Cram), 1908–11;
Gehron & Seltzer, renovation, 1955

Whereas Taylor is the heart of the Academy, Thayer Hall is its strength. When viewing the school from the river, or across the river, Thayer is what you see. Its monumental, locally quarried granite walls, replete with crenellated parapets, rise from the river and, as many have stated, seem to spring

Thayer Hall details

Thayer Hall

from the West Point rock itself. (For a terrific view and better notion of the scale, head across the river to Garrison. A charming village, it has kindly provided a public park directly opposite the Academy.)

Thayer, like many other West Point buildings, demonstrates that clever ability of the administrators and architects to create a structure that functions well on a variety of levels. Simply put: Thayer isn't just about having a gigantic granite wall so that viewers across the river can be impressed. Part of the 1903 competition, Thayer was built as a riding hall (on the grounds of the nineteenth-century riding hall). As such, it required a very large, uninterrupted open space inside. Cram made sure that it got what it needed. Horsemanship was taught in the building until the 1940s.

Equestrian skills were antiquated and eliminated from the curriculum not too long after the construction of Thayer Hall. In 1944 another competition was held that

Thayer Hall detail

Four gargoyles over the original entrance to Thayer Hall

included refurbishment of the Riding Hall. Delano & Aldrich won this competition but their plans were never acted upon. It wasn't until 1955 when Gehron & Seltzer's modifications were accepted that the building was radically altered for new needs. The interior was completely gutted and refitted for four floors of classroom space. It included the departments of math, military art, engineering, social sciences, law, ordnance, foreign languages, english, military psychology and leadership, and the bookstore. This is when its name was changed to Thayer Hall—to honor Sylvanus Thayer, affectionately referred to as the Father of the Academy.

Today, the inside gives not a clue as to the building's original function. Neither does the exterior. Modifications here have not been too damaging, but have managed to detract something from Cram's original

Thayer Hall detail

plan. The roof of the structure is now a parking lot; in order to provide proper safety for such a use, the parapets had to be raised a number of feet. This, of course, blocked more of the view of the river, something for which Cram's first design for this building was rejected. Additionally, Cullum Road was raised, and a number of pedestrian bridges built to span the space between Thayer and Taylor. The large entrances at which the bridges terminate were added in the 1955 renovation. The three wide original arena entrances have been filled in, thus leaving as the only clue to the building's original function five small grotesques that portray five uses of the horse. (These are above the entrance of the center portal.)

In spite of all these modifications, Thayer Hall still is an inspiring building. Its river-facing granite walls are little modified and lend that staggering sense of power and solidity to the Academy.

18. Power House (#604)

Cram, Goodhue & Ferguson (credited to Cram), 1905–09

The Power House is not one of the buildings a visitor would normally see—at least, not from the inside. It is deserving of a brief note as it was part of the 1903 competition and Cram managed to place it very close to the Academic Area without disturbing things. In other words it is a structure built for purely functional reasons that doesn't look like a purely functional building.

Cram placed the Power House just down from the edge of the bluff and right next to the Riding Hall (Thayer Hall, #601). In fact the two buildings are joined together in a small section at the southeast corner tower of Thayer Hall (which used to conceal a chimney stack). The Power House blends in well because Cram used the same granite as in Thayer, and he detailed the building similarly with a limestone string course, smaller versions of the stylized buttresses, and a crenellated parapet on

Power House

the southeast (river) side. From the river, the best and almost only view today, one would never guess this handsome structure provided power and heat for the campus.

The Power House was built to house a coal-fired generator. The steam produced was piped off to heat the buildings. Rail cars emerging from the rail tunnel delivered the coal, sent into the plant on a conveyor belt. Part of the mechanics of this operation were located in the tiny tower on the very southern tip of the building—Cram made sure even this received the granite facing and limestone trim of the larger building. In 1940 the generators were converted to oil.

Being a bit oddly shaped, the Power House building was carefully integrated into the steeply graded site. The Gothic style, unlike the classical, lends itself to this kind of picturesque accumulation of masses and heights. Cram fashioned the building according to the various parts required for its function and still managed to house it all in a manner fitting and suitable for the Academy.

19. West Point Club (#603)

McKim, Mead & White, 1901–1903; Gehron & Ross, addition, 1962

Originally the Officers' Mess and Quarters, this building was McKim, Mead & White's second and last project at the Academy. Stanford White, an exceptionally talented architect (and the firm's notorious New York collector, socialite, and womanizer), had in 1890 won a competition for a commemorative monument at the Academy. (Battle Monument, as it is called, is located on the eastern edge of the Plain.) White's connection with the Academy through his work on Battle Monument helped to win for the firm the commission for Cullum Hall (#605)—which in turn led to the firm's being invited

West Point Club

to design the Officers' Mess. Unlike Cullum this building was a less than satisfactory experience for the firm.

Complaints stemmed from the limited budget the government imposed for the project. More money was requested, and some was given, but when it was over, White griped that the building was "finished in a very meager way." Indeed, the Officers' Mess is not the most inspiring building on the campus; its budget of only $103,000 is to blame.

The structure is essentially a classical rectangle with regular fenestration—not the sort of stuff to get one's blood pumping. Warned that the firm would lose the contract if their costs were not brought down, they had to substitute a pale brick for the desired granite. (As if all of this weren't bad enough, in 1962 Gehron & Ross designed a huge, semicircular addition for the rear of the building that is simply detestable.)

What redeems this building, and does so grandly, is its bright and brilliant dining room. (Visitors can sneak a peek at the dining room but should remain considerate of diners.) The room abounds with classical detailing. All of the entrances/exits are finished with white trim that contrasts wonderfully with the pale yellow finish. Above the doors and running around the room are individual frieze panels. Atop the walls are rich, painted cornices. Most dramatically, yet with utter simplicity, is the room neatly halved, horizontally and vertically, with an entablature. This entablature "beam" is freestanding, supports a life-size figure of Athena above, and is supported in turn by two Doric columns. Continuing the lower cornice from the walls, the entablature also adds traditional Doric elements: triglyphs, guttae, and a Greek key pattern in the fascia. In something of a whimsical touch, the room also contains, on the fireplace mantel, small reproductions of Michelangelo sculptures from the Medici Chapel in Florence. (Personifications of Dawn and Twilight flank Giuliano de' Medici, which is odd as in the Medici Chapel it is Lorenzo who is flanked by Dawn and Twilight; Giuliano is flanked by Day and Night.)

McKim, Mead & White hoped the Academy would follow their lead and construct subsequent buildings in the classical style. They submitted a classical styled entry for the 1903 competition and hoped to pull the Academy away from Gothic or Tudor traditions. No doubt White thought he could pull this off with the sheer force of his personality, but the firm's proposal was too sweeping and took no notice of the school's history. (When Cram, Goodhue & Ferguson won, White thought their plan "the cheap carpenter's Gothic patch-work.") It is important to remember at this point, before the 1903 competition, no single style was utterly predominant on the campus. Additionally, McKim, Mead & White's buildings were, at the time, some of the largest structures on the campus. Although it is difficult to imagine now, the Academy's architectural style might have taken a classical turn and the campus grown into something quite other than what it is today.

Cullum Hall

20. Cullum Hall (#605) *McKim, Mead & White, 1895–1898; renovation, 1989*

This Memorial Hall I wish to be a receptacle of statues, busts, mural tablets, and portraits of distinguished deceased officers and graduates of the Military Academy, of paintings of battle scenes, trophies of war, and such other objects as may tend to give elevation to the military profession.

—Brevet Major General George W. Cullum

So reads a section of the will of Brevet Major General George W. Cullum, an 1831 graduate of the Academy, its sixteenth superintendent, and its first serious historian. Cullum had bequeathed $250,000 to build the structure, but it was more than his generous gift that made Cullum Hall (formerly Memorial Hall) such a success. Around 1850, when he was teaching engineering at the Academy, Cullum began publishing the Register of Officers and Graduates of the United States Military Academy. This and subsequent printings of the "Cullum Register" provided some of the first important historical documentation of the graduates of the Academy. Cullum himself worked on over three thousand entries. He thought it such an important endeavor that he also willed funds for later editions of the Register.

The building that satisfies Cullum's wishes is a dramatic, classical block sheathed in "pink" Milford granite. The front of the building features four partially engaged Ionic columns with a row of windows along the top of the columns. Above the columns is a frieze inscribed with "To the Officers and Graduates of the United States Military Academy." Along the cornice are evenly spaced lion heads. Around the building are a number of historic cannons, which the firm integrated into the plan of the building. Massive bronze doors at the main entrance are flanked by bronze pilasters—both of which are contained in a granite portal with pilasters and pediment. Facing the Plain, the facade of the building is clear, simple, and serious, the way a good classical building should be.

Cullum Hall

Around the back of the building McKim, Mead & White took advantage of the scenic possibilities by providing an open loggia running the length of the building. Visitors will want to stroll to this side of the building for delightful view of the Hudson River (and those more adventurous will want to attempt the steps down the slope below Cullum, which lead to Kosciuszko's Garden, one of the Academy oldest points of interest.)

Moving inside (sadly, closed to the public), one begins to grasp clearly the purpose of this building. The exterior of the building reflects something serious and noble; the interior is more intimate, more detailed. As a memorial building should be, it reflects the severity of the duty of military life (on the exterior) but charms us with personality and anecdote of the individual (on the interior). The main hall is flanked by painted columns and

Cullum Hall

Cullum Hall, interior

the ceiling, in many parts of the building, is elaborately detailed and/or painted. Downstairs is an assembly room and the hall of the building the latter displaying portraits of graduates, commemorative plaques, and various memorabilia. Filling the entire second floor is a massive ballroom. This latter space, well used in the past for dances and social activities, is festooned with giant Corinthian pilasters, plaster caryatids, rich classical detailing, and a frieze running around the room inscribed with the names of battles from the War of 1812 to the Spanish-American War of 1898. The ceiling features 340 rosettes, each holding a lamp. Like the hall below, this room too contains a myriad of significant memorabilia: flags, standards, weapons, maps, rare prints, medallions, miniatures, busts, bronzes, and more painted portraits.

Stanford White was very involved with all aspects of this building, albeit in an odd sort of way. McKim, Mead & White won the commission in 1893, just a few years after Stanford White had completed the Battle Monument for the Academy and even more recently completed of one of his best works, Gould Memorial Library for the City University of New York. White seemed to throw himself into the project, but from the start there was friction. Colonel Oswald H. Ernst, then superintendent, did not like the delays and management of the firm, and told them so. Strangely, White was apparently away for part of the time. The firm put Albert Ross, one of the assistants, in charge of the project.

After construction began White again threw himself into the work, designing various memorial items including some of the tablets, overseeing the room decorating and even continuing to work on the interior details for no charge to the Academy. But the firm's relationship with the Academy continued to be troubled. For unknown reasons in 1899 the firm was asked by the Academy to stop the job of furnishing the hall. (The job was given, in 1900, to the department store head John Wanamaker.) Professor Charles W. Larned, a key figure in the 1903 competition plan, asked White to pursue his "millionaire friends" in hopes of contributions for the building's collections; White refused. A serious problem came about when White misspelled "meritorious" in the frieze. The inscription's support holes had to be patched up. As if all of this weren't enough, one of the contractors leaked early drawings of the building to a pushy reporter, who published the following: "If the Cullum Memorial Hall at West Point turns out to be as squat and ugly as it appears in the plans it will be hard to make it worse." Charles McKim, who had been approached by the reporter earlier but refused to divulge any information, was furious. He wrote to Superintendent Ernst asking if they should "bring action against" the spurious contractor.

Despite all this, the building was finished and was very warmly received. Modifications have been few and mostly for safety. In 1976 a dramatic interior stairway was enclosed in wire glass. A detailed $1.7 million restoration was completed in 1989. All of the interior paint and gilding was refurbished and refreshed. The building no longer rooms officers nor does it house the Association of Graduates, but it is still used for various cadet activities (and for wrestling practice while cadets await the new gymnasium).

21. Lincoln Hall (#607)

Cram, Goodhue & Ferguson, 1908–09

The thoughtful viewer will realize a number of things about this building. It does not match the adjoining buildings much in style nor especially in coloring, it is placed ever farther along the edge of the Plain thus blocking more of the view, and it is an odd building with one part seemingly in a kind of dull classicism and the other in an equally dull Gothic.

Although it is hard to believe, this building was a part of Cram, Goodhue & Ferguson's 1903 plan. Originally it was built as a bachelor officers' quarters and today it functions as classroom and office space. It is a perfect example of a clever, and perhaps wise, idea executed with less than compelling results.

At the time of the 1903 competition, the Plain of the Academy was surrounded by a greater variety of buildings than today. To the west were the houses of the superintendent, the dean, the commandant, and faculty. Moving along the circle southward were Hunt's rugged Romanesque

Lincoln Hall

gymnasium, the simple Tudor Cadet (Central) Barracks, the very Doric
Cadet Chapel (now Cemetery Chapel), the Old Library (in something of a
Tudor/Norman look), and the classical Officers' Mess and Cullum Hall. It
was clear from the outcome of the competition that the style of the
Academy would progress in the rustic Gothic adopted by Cram, Goodhue &
Ferguson. This direction enshrined some of the oldest architectural tradi-
tions of the school, particularly the style embraced by the Old Library.
However, it presented a problem. What was to be done with the two build-
ings that had not only broken tradition with their siting on the edge of the
Plain but also by being in the classical style?

McKim, Mead & White's Officers' Mess and Cullum Hall were the
odd men out. Both were less than a decade old, both were well used, and
Cullum was well loved. They were good buildings. They were established
buildings. Cram, Goodhue & Ferguson's plan for the Academy had to incor-
porate these buildings. The solution was Lincoln Hall. Lincoln would be a
transitional structure, echoing something of the classicism of the Officers'
Mess and Cullum and of the rustic Gothic Cram, Goodhue & Ferguson sought
for the new buildings. Thus the portion of the building closest to its classical
neighbors is also a simple classical rectangle with little ornamentation, stylized buttresses, and regular fenestration. It would have fit in much more
effectively had a similar color of white brick been used instead of the buff.

A nicely towered section, in a style akin to the rustic Gothic of the
campus, is located on the eastern end of the building. Clearly not classical,
its massing and details signal to the viewer that something else is afoot.
Connecting the two structures is a narrow sort of hall, two stories, with windows on each story.

The building in many other settings would be a suitable, albeit unconventional, structure. Cram, Goodhue & Ferguson provided a rugged, granite lower level, a charming small balcony, and a small tunnel on the east side. For the Academy, however, the building is a failure as a transitional structure and contributes little to the campus. Fortunately, the large trees covering the front of the building distract one from realizing just how much of the river view is blocked.

22. USMA Library (#757)   *Gehron & Seltzer, 1964*

The USMA Library is an impressive edifice for something built in the aesthetically barren 1960s. Gehron & Seltzer were clearly sympathetic to the overall campus style of architecture as well as to the buildings immediately surrounding the Library. The ashlar granite facing matches well with Cret's addition (but less well with Cram, Goodhue & Ferguson's darker stone). While the structure itself is a relatively staid rectangle, it is the details that make it work. Stylized buttresses continue the fortress theme and break up the horizontal facade into vertical rhythms (and are similar to those of Bartlett on the north side). On the east corner of the building is a small tower featuring an eighteen-foot-tall sculpted figure of Athena. Along the crown of the building, instead of crenellations, the architects placed a suitable row of dentils. The north facade has a rugged arched center portal with leaded transom glass. It is the windows, however, that are the building's best feature.

USMA Library

Gehron & Seltzer kept the building from growing tedious with a variety of treatments. On the first floor are gently arched stone frames with modest tracery and leaded panes; this theme is repeated on the east facade fourth floor windows but on a slightly larger scale. In between, on the second and third floors, are much simpler windows in groups of three. For the north facade fourth floor, Gehron & Seltzer created what appears to be a continuous band of traceried windows. These are unique to the campus, are quite in the Gothic style, and act as a more delicate terminus of the wall, suitable for a library.

While this new Library was an appropriate companion for the Academy campus, what it replaced was much better. There are two great architectural tragedies at the Academy: the USMA Library and Eisenhower Hall. Although they produced different results in the end, they both required destruction of important older buildings. Tradition is clearly an important part of the Academy, one that it seeks to foster. Thus it is difficult to understand the decision that was made to destroy the Old Library.

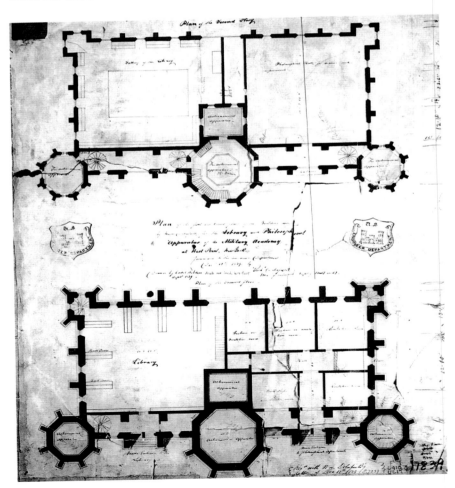

Plan of Old Library, Richard Delafield, drawing dated 1839

Interior of Old Library, Richard Delafield. Pictured in 1886 after restoration. Demolished.

Part of Major Richard Delafield's architectural contribution to the Academy was the Old Library. The Old Library was a part of Delafield's Tudor-Gothic vision for the campus. A charming and quirky building, it stood on the Plain for more than a hundred years. It was not terribly large, had three crenellated octagonal towers on the facade, leaded-glass, arched stone windows, and eventually was covered in ivy. Inside it was even better, like a Victorian parlor, with monumental fireplaces, traceried wood and glass bookshelves, and dozens of portraits. It served generations of Academy cadets.

Together with its neighbor, the Cadet Chapel (now Cemetery Chapel), these were two of the first architecturally significant works on the campus. More than mere stone and mortar, however, the Old Library seemed to symbolize much of the Academy's spirit. It housed the collection of books, of course, but also portraits of famous alumni. It was home to the superintendent's office and his staff. Up in the towers were the first astronomical instruments for the observatory. The department of natural and experimental philosophy lectured here. Like a great campus library should be, this Old Library was the heart and soul of the Academy. Choosing to destroy this irreplaceable building was a narrow and shortsighted decision.

23. Washington Hall (#745)

Arnold W. Brunner & Associates, William Gehron, Sidney F. Ross, William F. Pennell,
*   and Merle W. Alley, 1929;*
Delano & Aldrich, addition, 1946;
O'Connor & Kilham with Clarke & Rapauno, James Mongitore & Associates,
*   and Wisdopf & Pickworth, addition, 1965;*
O'Connor & Kilham, barracks addition, 1969

Three times a day the entire corps of cadets, more than four thousand students, marches into Washington Hall, sits down, and eats. The cadets do not wait in a cafeteria-style line, rather meals are served family style. The facilities required to operate food service on such a scale are tremendous. Washington Hall provides the space for those facilities and more. It is home to the food service areas, the dining area, and barracks and offices. Washington Hall is big. It is really, really big. (Sadly, the visitor will again be frustrated by not being allowed into the building.)

Prior to the construction of Washington Hall, mess was held in the old Grant Hall (demolished 1929, it stood where Grant Hall now stands). Meals were a formal occasion for cadets, replete with table linens, china, and servers. Dining was an even more formal occasion for officers; they enjoyed the above with crystal and silver. By 1926 it was clear that the old Mess would not suffice, so plans were arranged for a new hall. Nearly $2.5 million were spent on the original (1929) section of Washington Hall. Architects Brunner and associates designed a richly detailed Gothic hall, which functioned well for the nearly one thousand cadets. This building, which also held the cadet store and the drawing academy, was six stories

Washington Monument and Washington Hall

Washington Hall, front window

tall, had six sallyports on its main facade, and contained elegantly traceried windows at its center and south and west wings.

The first of the numerous additions was in 1946. To their credit Delano & Aldrich suggested a munificently subtle addition; their solution to the need for expansion was to add a very large, multistoried second building behind the first. While the kitchens were housed originally in a smaller structure behind Washington Hall, Delano & Aldrich's new building placed the kitchen facilities around a new dining wing. This solution was generous as it did not detract from the elegance of Brunner's building (excepting the loss of the lower sections of the traceried windows on the south and west wings). Delano & Aldrich's concern for the preservation of the original building was such that their addition called for the removal of twenty-six feet of rock from the hillside behind.

In 1965 another major addition was undertaken, this time with mixed results. O'Connor & Kilham planned for not only more dining space but also for barracks and classrooms. (Their 1969 addition was another entire wing providing mainly offices and more barracks off of the northeast wing.) This design doubled the size of Washington Hall by adding a new facade and the two wings. O'Connor & Kilham trumped Brunner by making

Washington Hall interior

their addition to the front of the building; now their facade would have the prestige of facing the Plain. There probably wasn't much choice as to which direction the building could expand and, in one of the most deft architectural moves at the Academy, the original facade was left intact on the interior.

Inside, the old facade, with its windows removed, acts as a brilliant centerpiece to the now incredibly large dining hall wings, creating one of the best interior spaces of the Academy. It is visible from its fourth floor down. On what was its first floor level is an open balcony referred to as the "poop

Washington Hall, mural by Tom Lofton Johnson

deck." It is from here that Cadet Adjutant can make announcements. It was from here that MacArthur made his famous "old soldiers never die" speech. Naturally, to create this sort of interior, much of the old building was lost. The original perpendicular stained glass window of the facade has been trimmed down and the top two floors are not visible from the inside (but oddly were left intact above the roof level and are visible from certain rooms at the top levels of Washington).

The interior today contains a wide assortment of details in addition to the older facade. The west windows of the west wing contain a very elaborate stained glass window by George Pearse Ennis. This work, completed in 1937, has 12,000 pieces and portrays the military life of George Washington. In the southeast wing is a stained glass window by the class of 1944 depicting famous American military battles. Artist Tom Lofton Johnson painted a large mural in 1936. Part of a WPA project, the mural is a montage of historic battles and military leaders. Johnson also planned for the myriad of flowers painted on the ceiling beams—these represent the countries that had colonized America. There are also numerous flags representing the states and provinces of America as well as paintings of significant army or Academy figures.

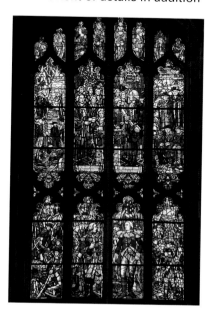

Washington Hall, Washington window by George Pearse Ennis

Outside, Washington Hall presents an impressive facade. Six stories in the wings and eight in the center, the building dominates the Plain but also embraces it. The building quite literally hugs the edge of the Plain. Its granite exterior hints at the style of the other buildings with a few crenellations and its towering center section, but overall is simpler and plainer. No doubt the old Washington facade was better, but having the new facade and wings of the building bend is a good and suitable solution to the space problem.

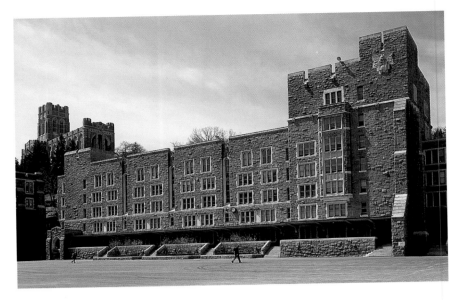

Scott Barracks

24. Scott Barracks (#735) *Paul Cret, 1938*

In many ways Paul Cret was the perfect choice for an Academy architect. Cret, French by birth, had served in World War I. After the war he enjoyed a career with many and varied commissions including a number of large institutional buildings, such as the Federal Reserve Building in Washington. Educated in the Beaux-Arts style, he was very much a traditionalist but with a penchant for streamlining. No doubt the Academy had these things in mind when they hired him.

This building will frustrate the visitor as it is not accessible nor is it easily visible; from the Plain only the top of a tower is visible. One can obtain a better view of the building from up above near the Cadet Chapel. (Renovations to the gymnasium may open up larger vistas of Scott.) Built on the site of an old Cadet Guard House, Scott Barracks features a more streamlined rustic Gothic style. Cret was very aware of what was brewing in the Bauhaus in the 1930s, and perhaps Scott Barracks reflects some of that simplicity. However, the addition of towers, stylized buttresses, sallyports, and embrasures belies the traditionalism that he sought for the Academy.

The embellishments are not grand but are enough. Vertical window bands help to break up the building's facade into more humanely scaled sections. There are a few sculptural elements: a limestone cadet head over the porch on the east side, an eagle and USMA shield on the northeast tower, a lion and griffin above the sallyport on the north side. The building itself is L-shaped with recessed corners on the north and south of the east facade. Scott is the first major building at the Academy to be constructed with reinforced concrete. (Nearly all of the Cram, Goodhue & Ferguson buildings are masonry supported.) It is sheathed in the same rustic granite quarried on the campus. Cret provided for variety on the exterior by allowing random stones to stick out from the wall.

Placement also is significant for Scott. Although barely visible from the Plain, the barracks does hold an important position behind Washington Hall (#745). With the addition to Washington called Eisenhower Hall, Scott Hall creates another useful courtyard space. And, with some excavation back into the hillside, Cret managed to place a very large building next to other important buildings—thus expanding the Academic Area without disturbing the Plain or extant buildings.

The building is five stories tall (seven in the northeast tower) and in keeping with the traditions of Academy housing, is divided up according to division, each inaccessible from the other. It was in one of the divisions in Scott that one of West Point's legends was born. In the evening of October 21, 1972, two plebes in room #4714 were visited by the shadowy figure of a nineteenth-century cavalryman with a handlebar mustache and musket. The plebes called for their captain who came and found the room "unusually cold." A navy midshipman later claimed responsibility but his story didn't hold up to scrutiny. The legend remains.

25. Arvin Gymnasium (#727)

Cram, Goodhue & Ferguson, 1906–10;
Edwin Dunstan, addition, 1935; Paul Cret, addition, 1938;
Delano & Aldrich, addition, 1946; Raymond & Rado, addition, 1967;
Sverdrup & Parcell & Associates, addition, 1975;
Sasaki Associates, renovation, 2005

Arvin Gym is a massive, sprawling, gigantic building with a history of additions and modifications. Perhaps here more than with any other building on the campus can the Acadamy's history be seen. Cram, Goodhue & Ferguson's 1910 gymnasium is the section one can see on the front, left facade. To its right is Edwin Dunstan's addition, and to its right is Raymond & Rado's addition. (The rest of the sections are behind and not normally accessible to visitors.)

The building, unlike any of the other academic structures, is built of brick. The brick helps the building blend with the three brick houses in front (those of the superintendent, commandant, and dean). It is also, of course, a much more economical material, an important factor in a structure of this size. Oddly, the additions, being slight variations on the rustic Gothic theme, help to give the building a smaller feel, as the facade is broken into the three sections.

Arvin Gymnasium

Two other gyms preceded Arvin. The first was the old Academic and Exercise Hall, or Academy, a fine, plain building with a few classical details, situated roughly where Taylor Hall is today. It was completed in 1838 and served until 1891, when it was demolished and Richard Morris Hunt began work on a new gym. Hunt was recruited by the Academy in order to lend a more consistent style to the campus. His gym was less Tudor or Gothic than Romanesque, with twin peaked towers and a massive arched entrance. It certainly was a rugged style and one perhaps more suited to the Academy's history. It fit in well with his other neighboring building, Pershing Barracks (#751)—Hunt's only extant work at the Academy.

In only nine years it became evident that the Academy would again need more room. Professor Charles W. Larned, a key figure in the Academy's architectural story, proposed enlarging Hunt's gym, suggesting some stylistic variations to bring it back to Tudor— what he considered West Point's "keynote" style. Instead a new gym was included on the list of needed buildings for the 1903 competition. When Cram, Goodhue & Ferguson's

Arvin Gymnasium

gym was completed, there were 417 cadets; by 1931 there were at least 1,000. And so it went, as with all of the Academy, expansion after expansion, building more and larger buildings. Indeed, the present gym complex is now undergoing a massive renovation by Sasaki Associates of Boston. At a current cost of $75.5 million, the renovated gym will be a gigantic, 370,000 square-foot, five-story complex. It is slated for completion in 2005. Although constructed of brick, the renovated gym is to blend stylistically with the surrounding buildings. Fortunately, many of the earlier historic facades will be retained.

26 | Catholic Chapel
27 | Jewish Chapel
28 | Water Treatment Plant
29 | Cadet Chapel
30 | Chaplain's Quarters
31 | Herbert Hall

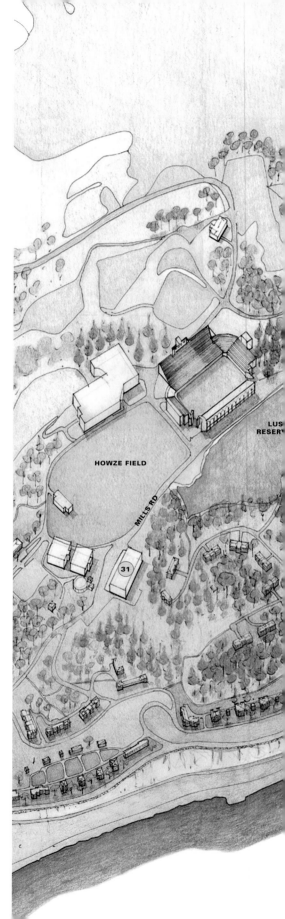

LUS
RESER

HOWZE FIELD

MILLS RD

31

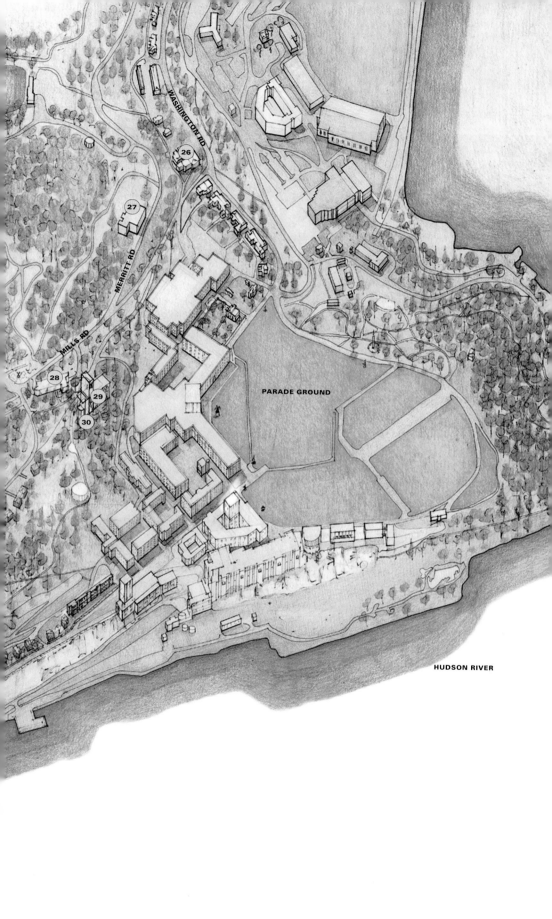

WASHINGTON RD

MERRITT RD

MILLS RD

26

27

28

29

30

PARADE GROUND

HUDSON RIVER

God and West Point

Religion has always been an important part of the United States Military Academy. From the time of West Point's founding, cadets were required to attend weekly chapel (until this was challenged in court in 1969). Services often followed the Episcopal Church format but were tamely nonsectarian. Army Chief Engineer General Joseph Swift suggested to the army that "the service of that church was deemed to be the most appropriate to the discipline of a military academy." Discipline was thought key to a young man's education. Sylvanus Thayer, superintendent from 1817 to 1833, much in keeping with other nineteenth-century pedagogy, was convinced that one needed character to develop the body, mind, and soul. The best way to achieve this was by immersion in a particular kind of environment. Religion—Christianity really—was to contribute to the environment.

Compulsory chapel attendance was not always met with joy. Cadets complained about chapel from the beginning, but for a variety of reasons. Cadet Cullum, patron of Cullum Hall, disliked the uncomfortable, backless benches and the dull sermons; Cadet Grant did not like the fact that the service was Episcopalian, nor that he had to march to get there. On the other hand, chapel did provide a brief occasion for the use of chewing tobacco, protected as the cadets were from their superiors. Once, at least, the cadets were requested to stop chewing, and spitting, as it polluted the floor for other services. In 1858 Cadet Emory Upton stated what many were most likely thinking when he wrote that the Academy "is a hard place to practice religion; though few scoff at it, yet a great majority totally disregard it."

Many at the Academy, however, have regarded religion very carefully. There has certainly been enough interest that it was felt suitable to construct a number of costly buildings for religious edification. Currently on the campus there are five operating chapels for cadets and/or enlisted men. These include three on this Walk and two more, the Cemetery Chapel (or Old Cadet Chapel) and the Post Chapel, in the Enlisted Men's Area. In addition, there are a number of other religious groups represented on campus that don't have buildings of their own. For example, Eastern Orthodox Christians hold services in the crypt of the Cadet Chapel.

Why is it then that despite a history of complaints from cadets and a skeptical culture the Academy still fosters religion among the students? No doubt some of the support must come from the ever present sense of tradition. It seems, however, that there must be a deeper and more powerful reason. What drives some to lay down their lives for others is a belief in transcendence. A potent materialistic atheism urges certain action in those who embrace it, but dying for others usually isn't one of them. To fight as a soldier, to be the one who could very well die in battle, requires that one believe in some purpose, some meaning in reality. It has often been remarked that there are no atheists in foxholes. Perhaps this maxim has less to do with fear of what one might encounter in death than how one might find meaning in fighting. Certainly, the Academy urges cadets to think seriously about why they study warfare, why they might have to lay down their lives. The Academy recognizes that religion has a role to play in defining that meaning.

26. Catholic Chapel (#699) *Heins & LaFarge, 1900*

Mandatory Protestant chapel attendance was the tradition for cadets at the Academy, regardless of creed. It was certainly fine for a cadet to embrace Judaism or Catholicism, and to worship, but the only official building for worship was the Cadet Chapel on the hill. Roman Catholic cadets did not have a structure of their own, despite the fact that the local diocese had been wanting to build one for years. In the late nineteenth century, the very capable and persuasive Father C. G. O'Keefe was put in charge of wresting permission for a building. The Secretary of War gave permission in 1897, only to have it revoked by the next administration. In 1898 the issue was argued before Congress and permission was given. Construction began almost immediately.

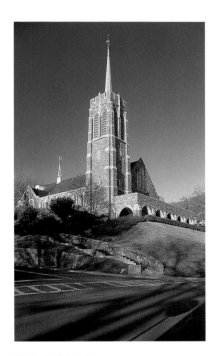

Catholic Chapel

O'Keefe had been thinking about this chapel for years. During a trip to England, he was inspired by a visit to the Abbey Church of St. Ethelreda in Essex. The church had been constructed by thirteenth-century Carthusian monks and converted to Protestant use by Queen Elizabeth. O'Keefe made a sketch of the church in hopes that it would serve as the model for a West Point chapel. When the project was approved, the young firm of Heins & LaFarge was hired. They are known for their work at the New York City Zoo, the tile work in some of the subways stations, the Cathedral of St. Matthew in Washington, and the monumental Cathedral of St. John the Divine in New York (with a nave that was later completed by Ralph Adams Cram). Their work on the Catholic Chapel was very close to how Father O'Keefe had imagined it.

Catholic Chapel and Hudson River

The chapel sits on a dramatic site, one chosen by O'Keefe, with good views of the river and in turn offering good views of itself. Constructed also of the locally quarried granite and trimmed in limestone, the chapel blends in well with the campus. It is a simply massed, steeply pitched building with a square bell tower on the east side of the narthex.

The exterior has been modified in a few ways. As priests were offered no housing at the Academy, it was decided to construct a rectory in 1933. This low building, connected to the west side of the chapel by a short hall, helps to create a much more interesting space when approaching the chapel. The exterior space was again improved by an expansion in 1957. This project required more exterior granite.

As the Academy retained some control over the project, and desired that the structure fit in with the rest of the campus, it appeared that finding the right kind of granite would be a problem; the original portion of the chapel was faced in granite that had been weathered for fifty years. In a very simple and thoughtful gesture, the Academy offered the granite Old Observatory, condemned since 1946, to the highest and only bidder, the Catholic Chapel. Stone problem solved, the facade of the chapel was extended for a larger foyer, an ambulatory below and porch above added, the tower modified to its current shape, and two more doors were added to the front.

The interior of the chapel has gone through many changes. Most of the changes have been to the color and style of the furnishings. Originally the floor was a simple black and white tile and the altar was of marble. The most dramatic alteration has been the addition of painted designs to the exposed beams of the ceilings and walls. Added throughout the chapel's history, the stained glass windows depict various saints with military connections. St. Stephen is portrayed holding a replica of the new chapel.

The Catholic Chapel has had the privilege of being the first Roman Catholic Chapel built on government property. It was the only structure on the entire campus that was not owned by the government. In 2000, ownership of the chapel grounds and buildings was assumed by the Academy.

27. Jewish Chapel (#750) *Max Abramovitz, 1984*

For many years Jewish cadets had to worship in the Cadet Chapel, and then later in a chemistry lab. Perhaps inspired by the neighboring Catholic Chapel, in 1968 Jewish alumni from the Academy organized themselves for the purposes of raising funds to construct a Jewish Chapel. Like Catholic alumni Jewish alumni also felt a strong historical connection with the Academy and pointed out that some of the first Academy graduates were Jewish. The impetus to build was evinced by the rapid raising in a few years of $6 million, all from private donations.

Max Abramovitz of Harrison & Abramovitz, involved in design projects at the United Nations, Philharmonic Hall of Lincoln Center, and Brandeis University, was hired. In the early 1970s Abramovitz worked up the designs, which were approved by the planning advisory board (under the same 1898 Congressional Act that had approved construction of the Catholic Chapel). There were high hopes for the building. Some thought it would be "the most visited Jewish building in the nation."

Jewish Chapel

Constructed of the same ashlar granite as the Cadet Chapel, the Jewish Chapel design was to be consistent with the style of the rest of the Academy. Clearly the only thing consistent with the rest of the campus is the use of granite. Traditionalist architects were hard to come by in the 1970s and this building demonstrates that. Abramovitz had difficulty finding anyone who could design in the Gothic style. He eventually used a Ukrainian draftsman in his office who had been trained in Europe and had some knowledge of the style. Sadly, his knowledge was not enough to create more than this slab-sided monolith.

Fortunately, the chapel is redeemed by its thoughtful and warm interior spaces; it is one of the few Academy buildings that is actually better on the inside than the out. The visitor is first lulled into a quiet courtyard Memorial Garden for a moment's repose before entering the intimate lobby. Inside the ceilings are relatively low, the lighting soft, and the visitor urged to explore the manifold objects in the gallery space. The library and seminar room serve to teach about Jewish contributions to American history, military and otherwise. Progressing along the gallery, one passes a tiny courtyard that produces soft illumination for the hall, and then arrives at a skylit vestibule to the sanctuary. Surrounded by floors of polished stone and walls of brush-hammered concrete, one enters this space through a dark, wood screen. The screen continues up the back wall and along the ceiling with close-set wooden ribs, warming up the chilly, gray concrete. Light also warms the tall room, pouring gently in from the east facing windows at the altar end, from the hidden fluorescent tubes above the wooden ceiling, and from the small etched windows on the side walls. The Messusah Case, the Ark, the Bema, and the etched bronze tablets on the facade of the building were all created by artist Sidney Simon.

28. Water Treatment Plant (#726)   *Office of the Quartermaster, 1932*

Situated where it is, just adjacent to the Cadet Chapel, this building is sure to raise some questions in the mind of the visitor. It is, in fact, nothing more than a mundane water treatment facility. What makes it stand out, apart from its location, is its fine use of granite and stone trim and its odd massing. The latter comes from the way in which the building has been integrated into the hillside. It is a handsome building and appears more important than it really is. This, of course, is the whole point and one for which the architects and administrators should be applauded; it is an important structure by virtue of its location next to the chapel. A significant detriment to the area would have been caused had this plant been constructed of brick. As it is, rendered in the rustic Gothic of its neighbor, the visitor

Water Treatment Plant

assumes it to have some function associated with the chapel. It is another good example of the Academy, with some thought, turning pedestrian facilities into attractive buildings that contribute to the campus.

29. Cadet Chapel (#722)

Cram, Goodhue & Ferguson (credited to Goodhue), 1906–10

The building that goes beyond the call of functional duty and is, without a doubt, the most beautiful and noteworthy building on the Academy campus, is the Cadet Chapel. Lending a loftiness to the campus, its silhouette creates one of the best known views of the Academy and the site. It is a prime example of a building with all factors in its favor: materials, composition, construction, siting, landscaping, and ornament. It works on every level and does just what it is supposed to do: manifest the spiritual goals of the Academy. Scholar Bethanie C. Grashof put it this way:

> Its location on the hillside overlooking the Plain and the remainder of the academic core is befitting a church of this magnitude. If the Administration Building is the epitome of military strength, then the Chapel could be considered the epitome of spiritual strength. Just as the Gothic Cathedral was built in an important part of a city and was visible for miles around, so too is the Cadet Chapel as it reaches up out of the granite hillside.

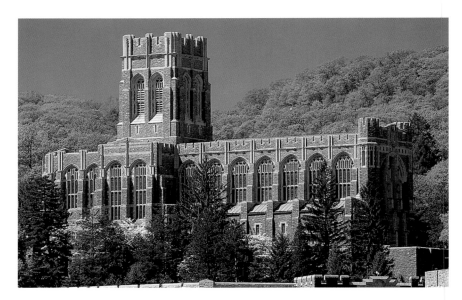

Cadet Chapel

Thanks to Cram's skill, the chapel was constructed on the hillside behind Washington Hall, not on the eastern edge of the Plain as some in the administration desired. Thanks to Goodhue, the Academy received a nearly pure example of Gothic church building. The flexibility of the Gothic style permitted Goodhue to deftly manipulate ornamental details, lending them a militaristic edge. It also provided numerable opportunities for various Class projects in providing the requisite interior components: stained glass windows, altar furnishings, interior decor, pipe organ. Thus, in one stunning move, the school was blessed with a spectacularly sited chapel, stylistically suited to the campus, and ready for contributions toward the abundant interior details that would make the chapel its own.

Goodhue's work follows closely that of Cram, who was well known for his church design, as well as the English team of Bodley & Garner and their American counterpart, Henry Vaughan. All were attempting to instill new life into traditional Gothic forms; all were quite successful in doing so, often by utilizing modern building techniques, less extravagant materials and ornamentation, and by building on a smaller scale. Proponents of the Gothic Revival were attempting to revive the implicit values manifested in the forms while at the same time aiming toward a more realistic affordability.

Certainly Goodhue was after some of the same ends here; at $487,000, while expensive, the Cadet Chapel (and Chaplain's Quarters) was reasonable for what was achieved. Goodhue began with a simple and very traditional cruciform building. Over the crossing is a square, English-styled tower with belfry; flanking the narthex portal are two hexagonal towers. While the towers are typical embellishments, Goodhue designed them with atypical crenellated parapets. There is also a line of crenellations along the top of the walls at roof level. These simple touches are what lend the militaristic style to the building (and also saved quite a bit in the cost by eliminating the usual stone towers and finials).

The structure itself is traditional. Cram & Goodhue were genuinely attempting to revive much of the Gothic tradition; the dark, granite walls of the chapel carry the load without the benefit of steel girders, and the tower is built to carry the weight of the twelve-bell chime housed within. However, in a very suitable modern move, Goodhue did use steel trusses to support the roof deftly hidden up above the nave vaulting. These, while not orthodox, saved a great deal of time and money without altering the appearance of the chapel.

On the exterior of the building are a variety of subtle details in keeping with the Gothic tradition. Both the tower and the nave walls have a stringcourse with figures sculpted by Lee Lawrie (under direction from Goodhue). The tower features a variety of humorous figures, one with bucket and brush, one with a broom, a soldier with books, and musicians.

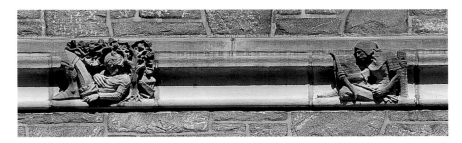

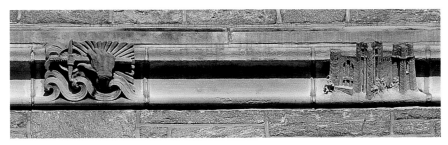

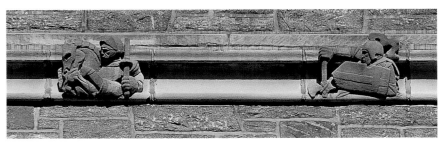

Cadet Chapel, west side details

Cadet Chapel, sword/cross over central entrance

The west nave walls feature Arthurian figures: jousting knights, knights with arms, Sir Galahad, Camelot. On the northwest tower are King Richard, Joan of Arc, Elaine, and Lancelot. On the east nave walls, starting on the north facing tower, are St. George with the dragon and a variety of medieval and Arthurian figures; the last two of these displays a knight's armor and the Holy Grail, symbolizing the end of the battle and its reward.

The north facade features a main portal divided by two buttresses. Above the north window is a shield with cross and a scroll which reads, "Quis ut Deus." ("Who is like God?") These refer to the Archangel Michael. Above the door is a huge sword of stone, perhaps Excalibur, oriented like a cross. On the hinges of the wooden door is a Latin inscription which translated reads: "O God, who does crush out war and by whose powerful defense defeats the assailants of them that trust in You, come to the help of Your servants who beg Your mercy."

The north side of the chapel is fronted by the Galilee Porch, similar to those found in some English cathedrals. In the Middle Ages this space was reserved for penitents. Below this level, as one heads along the stairs down the hill, is an iron barred door, a hint of medieval ecclesiastical dungeons. Finally, the observant visitor will notice that surrounding the chapel are very large cedar and pine trees. These must have been part of the landscape program laid out by Frederick Law Olmsted, America's first landscape architect and the designer of Central Park. Cedar and pine trees, evergreens, have a long history of Christian symbolism for eternal life.

Moving inside the building the visitor will be surrounded by a wealth of richness and detail, color and light, exactly as one should find in a Gothic church. Floor materials increase in value as one progresses toward the altar: concrete in the narthex, granolitic in the nave and transept, slate and Welsh quarry tile in the chancel, Mercer tiles in the altar area, and hardwood in the sacristy. In the crossing floor is a special removable section that provided access to the vaulted crypt below. (Planned for important persons, this crypt was never used as such.) Above the narrow side aisles are the magnificent stained glass windows. Willet Stained Glass Window & Decorating won the commission, beating out Tiffany. It is thought that Cram had something to do with this selection, as he detested the opalescent glass popular at the time and wanted to return to the more traditional Gothic

Cadet Chapel, "Duty," "Honor," "Country" panels of south window

translucent glass. Each year's graduating class contributed one window panel for itself and another in honor of the class that graduated 100 years earlier, until all the windows were completed in 1976. These windows portray scenes and figures from the Bible. The window over the entrance was installed in 1923 as a memorial to Academy graduates who perished in World War I. Its theme is the triumph of Christ over sin and death. The Sanctuary Window, the first installed, was built "To the Glory of The God of Battles and in Faithful Memory of the Departed Graduates of the United States Military Academy" and features various heroes of Christianity. All of the stained glass windows were removed, cleaned, releaded, and replaced during 1998–1999.

There are many other details, only a handful of which can be mentioned here. (Visitors are encouraged to take their time in exploring the building.) In the tenth row of pews, on the left side, the visitor will find a candle burning perpetually, a memorial to those soldiers missing in action. The first pew on the right is the superintendent's. On the railing in front of this pew are small signature plates from each of the Academy's superintendents; the current superintendent's plate is on the armrest. At the intersection of the nave and transepts, atop the piers which support the arches, are charming corbel sculptures of the apostles and virtues. Much smaller sculptures can be found in the "chapel" areas: an angel with a lamp symbolizing wisdom and an angel with an hourglass symbolizing temporality.

The delicately carved wooden choir stalls lead the visitor toward the altar, which is carved from a single block of marble. Behind the altar is the carved reredos featuring the Archangel Michael battling a dragon.

Cadet Chapel, east side of nave

Paneling flanking the reredos features shields with symbols of events and persons of the Old and New Testaments. To the left of the altar Goodhue added the Lepers' Squint, a feature borrowed from medieval cathedrals. These small window slots, usually located near the narthex, were used to view the mass by those not allowed to enter. Here Goodhue has placed it so that the chaplain may view the altar from a hidden room above the sacristy. Iconographic symbols are found on the hand-painted tiles on the floor of the sanctuary. The rug in front of the altar was given to the Academy by Ethiopian Emperor Haile Selassie during a visit in 1953. And although out of sight, the twelve-bell chime in the tower was cast by the Meneely Bell Company of Troy, New York, in 1919. It is played from a traditional "pumphandle" chimestand located below the belfry.

The organ at the Cadet Chapel is the largest of any church in the world. (There do exist, however, a few larger organs put to secular use.) A full-time organ curator maintains the more than 20,000 pipes hidden throughout the building, up in the nave galleries, under the seats of the transept galleries, and in the upper spaces flanking the altar behind the visible pipes (which are just for looks and do not function).

30. Chaplain's Quarters (#60)

Cram, Goodhue & Ferguson (credited to Goodhue), 1908–10

The prestigious appointment of chaplain at West Point, made on a rotating basis, is made all the more sweet because of the Chaplain's Quarters. Tucked neatly behind the Cadet Chapel, the house was built at the same time and in the same granite. Remaining out of view of most visitors, the house is set at an angle behind the chapel. Goodhue gave the house a varied massing, which keeps the viewer interested and exploring. Particularly dramatic is the two-story bay window on the west side of the house. (It illuminates the stairway inside.) The house is quite large, with six bedrooms (which includes the servant's quarters), a formal dining room, a parlor, and library. Atop the house are three granite chimney stacks that provide flues for fireplaces in most rooms.

Chaplain's Quarters

The house is filled with many rich features. A number of rooms have exposed beams and many windows are leaded. The first floor has oak paneling with double dovetail pegs and decorative plaster ceilings. In the dining room one finds linen-fold oak paneling and a vaulted and decorated plaster ceiling. The best feature of the house, and one visitors will not be seeing, are the two secret passages. The potential benefits of placing the Chaplain's Quarters right next to the Cadet Chapel were not lost on Goodhue. Off the second floor chaplain's dressing room, behind a closet door, is a hidden room that leads to a small vestibule from which the chaplain may peer through the Leper's Squint in the chapel. Even more delightful is the hidden bookcase door in the first floor library. One of the sections of the built-in bookcases is hinged and leads to a passage that opens into the chapel sacristy.

31. Herbert Hall (#698) *Quinlivan, Pierik & Krause, 1995*

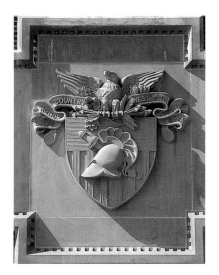

Herbert Hall detail

Herbert Hall, named for James K. Herbert, an alumnus (1930), is one of the newest buildings at the Academy. It is home to the Association of Graduates and was completely funded through their efforts. Herbert Hall exemplifies the success a building can attain despite many obstacles.

No doubt, Herbert Hall is off the beaten path. It is sited neither near the Plain nor any important architectural group on campus. Located south from the Academic Area and Cadet Chapel, Herbert Hall is situated just below Lusk Reservoir's retaining wall. Herbert uses this as an advantage; the weighty, granite wall rises up as a backdrop to the parking lot. Besides the wall, there is a very steep hillside rising behind the entire building. Rather than ignoring or ramming the building up against it, the architects have designed a pleasant brick terrace with benches and a fountain, the Alumni Plaza, between the building and the verdant hillside—encouraging visitors to view the interesting and varied terrain. The rear of the building is detailed, as well, not a plain side that faces a parking lot. The building was meant to be seen from this side, too.

The front facade of the building presents an odd face. There is so much going on one isn't quite certain what to make of it. Still, with the vast array of gables and windows, arches and doorways, one can glimpse something of the Academy style. The building is brick but has good stone detailing, particularly in the balcony above the main entrance. Its contrast with the darker brick reminds one of Cram, Goodhue & Ferguson's buildings on the Academic Area. There are also a smattering of crenellation and arches.

Inside the main entrance, one finds a paneled oval foyer donated by the Class of 1964. This ovoid space extends up to a balcony level on the

Herbert Hall

second floor, creating a very open and dynamic view. The entire southern end of the building houses the two-story great hall. Ready for alumni gathering, this large and inviting space is broken up into a variety of smaller, more intimate areas. Herbert Hall demonstrates that contemporary architecture can, in fact, suitably compliment the Academy's traditional style while remaining functional and economical.

Academy Housing and Enlisted Men's Area

32 | Superintendent's Quarters
33 | Commandant's Quarters
34 | Dean's Quarters
35 | Professors' Row
36 | Family Housing
37 | Quarters
38 | Cemetery Chapel
39 | Enlisted Men's Family Quarters
40 | Enlisted Men's Family Quarters
41 | Enlisted Men's Family Quarters
42 | Enlisted Men's Family Quarters
43 | Religious Education Facility
44 | Switch Station
45 | Post Chapel

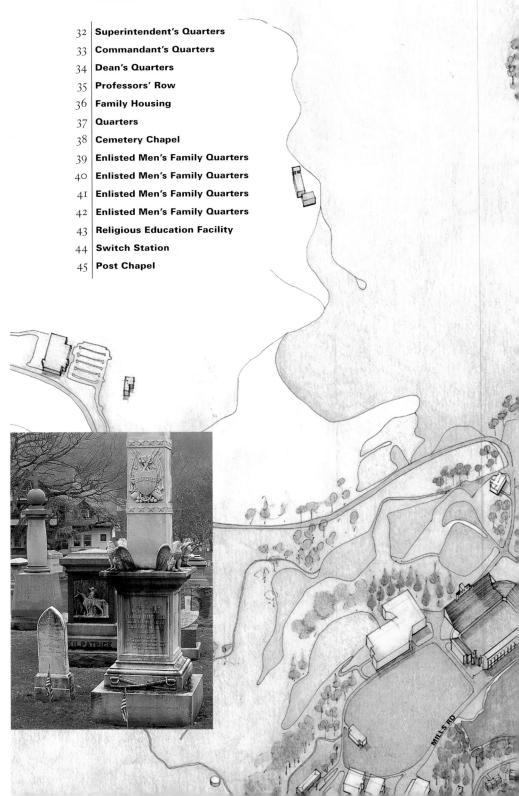

TARGET HILL
ATHLETIC FIELD

41

40

43

39

45

42

CEMETERY

38

MERRITT HILL RD

WASHINGTON RD

UPTON RD

HUDSON RIVER

37

WASHINGTON RD

36

35

MERRITT RD

34

33

32

PARADE GROUND

Living at West Point

This Walk actually comprises two distinct areas. The first visits a number of houses, beginning with that of the superintendent and ending with a small group of faculty houses on Washington Road. Where this group ends, near the cemetery, is where the historic Enlisted Men's Area—the second section of the Walk—begins.

Many visitors to the United States Military Academy are unclear as to exactly what is located at the Point. In addition to the Academy, there is a very large support staff operated by the United States Army. This staff contains a very broad variety of military personnel from cooks to ordnance supervisors. One portion of the campus where these people live, the Enlisted Men's Area, is the active part of the military base, the oldest continuously operating military base in America.

Of course West Point was first founded as an army base for Revolutionary forces. Perched on the Hudson, the terrain was very favorable for defense as well as for the monitoring of river traffic. There was little military action seen at the Point, and after the War of 1812 the defensive mission of the Point lessened. From this period on the military post grew into a support structure for the Academy.

This area for the enlisted men grew up north of the Plain for practical reasons; there was a north dock for loading and unloading supplies. In the first half of the nineteenth century it was a simple area called Camp Town. An 1844 guidebook describes it thus:

> A pleasant road passes through Camp Town but there is nothing particularly attractive in the appearance of the village. It is inhabited chiefly by private soldiers, and by laborers connected with the Academy. It contains the barracks of the musicians and soldiers, the magazine, a number of mechanics' shops, and the cavalry stables.

Cadets did not live in the Enlisted Men's Area; they have always been separated at the Point. By 1865 there was a distinct effort to more clearly separate the enlisted from the academic portions of the Academy. The houses that line Washington Road may have represented a conscious effort to keep the areas separate but still linked. Certainly, they act as a buffer between the sections.

Decade by decade more and more housing was constructed. This reached a kind of climax in 1890 with the construction of the long awaited Enlisted Men's Hospital, centrally located in the area. In 1899, however, there was an effort to lower the numbers of enlisted men. The report of visitors for that year listed four reasons why: soldiers and their families were the source of infectious diseases, the cost of larger housing for soldiers and their families was draining Academy funds, enlisted housing areas could be better used for Academy purposes, and the provision of married quarters could only increase the potential for cadets marrying. The report made little difference and the Academy, and thus the area, continued to grow to such a point that by the 1960s there was no space left. In 1964 a new Enlisted Men's Area was begun to the southwest of the campus with a request for 200 new houses. In spite of this expansion housing still remains at a premium on the campus.

With its very large trees and distinctive vistas, this part of the campus is best enjoyed by foot. It is suggested that the visitor begin at the Superintendent's House, continue along the sidewalk past Professors' Row, down past the Cram, Goodhue & Ferguson houses, and into the Cemetery Chapel and grounds. The large Enlisted Men's Area is best seen by automobile.

32. Superintendent's Quarters (#100)

Attributed to Office of the Quartermaster, c. 1819; Paul Cret, alterations, 1930–1938

The simplicity of this house belies its vast importance in the history of the Academy. Every superintendent since Sylvanus Thayer has lived in this house; nearly every American president since then has entered this house. It is the oldest extant building on campus (excepting Fort Putnam, of course). Originally, it was designed with a basement that was to provide office space for the superintendent, his adjutant, and an orderly. Today it is home to the superintendent and his family.

Typical of many Federal-style homes, the house consists of a basic rectangle with two floors (and basement) and features a central hall

Superintendent's Quarters

Superintendent's Quarters

configuration. There have been many additions to the house, most of them difficult to date. The last major alterations to the house, which included extending the (added) porch, were done in the 1930s by architect Paul Cret.

     Cram, Goodhue & Ferguson in their 1903 plan wanted to demolish the house and provide for the superintendent a much larger and more stately home on the eastern edge of the Plain. Outcry from the community preserved the house; it was too treasured a piece of history. Today it stands, with the neighboring Dean's Quarters and Commandant's Quarters, in odd disharmony with the massive facades of Arvin Gym and Washington Hall.

     The Superintendent's Quarters now acts as a kind of microcosm of the Academy, and perhaps the nation. It is no longer an original building, having been layered with so many additions and improvements. But, like the campus at large, underneath the layers of history is a very much remembered and revered past. The house is modest, to be sure, but some of the most important figures in American and world history have passed through its doors. On the south side of the house is a walled garden, another microcosm, which features plants from all fifty states. Both house and garden suggest a lack of pretense and a wealth of opportunity—ideals most Americans treasure.

33. Commandant's Quarters (#101)

Attributed to Office of the Quartermaster, 1821

This house was constructed at the same time as was the Superintendent's Quarters and has always been home to the Commandant of the Academy. It too began as a simple Federal-style rectangle and was also modified through the years with various additions and improvements. The first porch was added in 1855 and the room additions began in 1867. It is unclear if the building was originally painted, whitewashed, or just plain brick.

Inside, the home features some nice details, including plaster moldings in the parlors and dining room and marble mantels over the fireplaces. A dramatic arch separates the entry hall and the stair hall.

Commandant's Quarters

34. Dean's Quarters (#102)   *Q. A. Gilmore, 1857*

The Dean's Quarters is stylistically distinct from its neighbors, the Superintendent's Quarters and the Commandant's Quarters. The difference reflects the change in architectural taste in the mid-nineteenth century, which was due, in very large part, to the work of Andrew Jackson Downing. Downing was a horticulturist and is often credited with being the Father of the American Park. He wrote a number of influential books with the assistance of architect A. J. Davis, including *Cottage Residences* (1842) and *The Architecture of Country Houses* (1850). These books, targeting a middle-class audience, were immensely popular; filled with plans and drawings, they were also practical. A champion of the picturesque in landscape design, Downing in these books instructed the reader how one could build, or modify, in what became known as the Carpenter Gothic style. And he lived just up the road in Newburgh, New York.

While the Dean's Quarters does not follow Downing's precepts exactly, his influence is clear. The shape of the cottage is typical Downing, with a symmetrical facade of three bays, two-and-one-half stories tall, with porch. The visitor should be able to pick out the "Gothic" elements: pointed arched center window and openings, steep protruding gable, wooden "tracery" under the eaves. The house has been maintained to its original appearance with the exception of the protruding wings on the rear of the structure. (The east wing is contemporary with the house but was not originally connected.) Most likely the house was not originally painted, and its roof may have been metal rather than its current slate. Downing, however, did offer directions for both painting the exterior and using slate in his books.

Dean's Quarters

Professors' Row

35. Professors' Row (#103, 105, 107)

Attributed to Office of the Quartermaster, 1828

In June 1828 Daniel Corwin was paid $12,339.50 for the construction of "two double stone houses to be erected by contract at West Point." What the Academy received were two very simple houses, rectangular in shape, of local granite. (Building #107 was the first and acted as model for the others.) Red limestone window sills and quoins added color to the buildings. Each home was to house two families. The original portion of the structure is still clearly evident as the center of each house.

These buildings have seen many alterations, some of them receiving as many as eight separate additions over the years, reflecting something of the history of architectural taste in America. The visitor may look for elements of Greek Revival, Italianate, and shingle styles in the additions. Certainly Building #107's mansard-roof addition is a stand out.

Inside one finds a variety of nice detailing. Some have patterned wood floors, many rooms have plaster cornices, and some have rosette paterae. These houses came to be filled with some of the most illustrious professors of the Academy. For obvious reasons they remain some of the Academy's most sought-after housing.

Family Housing for Company Grade and Warrant Officer

36. Family Housing for Company Grade and Warrant Officer (#109)
Standard Quartermaster design, 1875

This massive three-story house may be a very early example of military housing based on standardized quartermaster plans. It appears very similar to houses that were built around 1890 at Fort Wood and Governors Island in New York. Not much has been altered; the basic shape of the house remains a cross. The white trim is probably incorrect. Most likely it was darker, such as is seen in other late nineteenth-century houses, in an attempt to imitate brownstone (which does trim the sills and lintels).

There are some odd features of the house that reflect, like so many other Academy buildings, changing styles. The gables on the south, east, and west sides are all in the Greek Revival style while that to the north is Gothic. A heavy wood cornice and large Italianate brackets support the wooden eaves. On the south side is a small oriel window.

While the house was designed for a single officer's family, it has now been modified to house four families. As built, the basement contained the laundry, storeroom, water closet, and kitchen, the first floor the front and back parlors and a dining room. Above, the second and third floors contained bedrooms and a bath. Today, after the modifications, two housing units are located on the basement and first floor, two more on the second and third floors.

37. Quarters (#116, 118, 120, 122)

Cram, Goodhue & Ferguson, 1908

As with Cram, Goodhue & Ferguson's other quarters (Buildings #21–48), these four houses are the best available on the campus. These duplexes are distinctively shaped, lavishly appointed, surrounded by trees, and have spectacular views of the Hudson. None of these houses is identical, but they all share some similar characteristics on both the exterior and interior. (This group of houses is not identical to Buildings #21–48, although they share some very similar exterior characteristics.)

For the exterior Cram, Goodhue & Ferguson provided a variety of gables and projections that give the buildings much movement and the appearance of being asymmetrical (which they are not). Oddly spaced fenestration contributes to the effect. The walls are load-bearing brick but the structure does have some steel to help support the unusual loads. Limestone and bluestone trim are used to good effect, particularly in the caps on the "buttresses," which remind the viewer of the more monumental structures just down the road. While the houses are not what one would term Gothic, or even Carpenter Gothic, like the Dean's Quarters (Building #102), they certainly aren't classical either. Cram, Goodhue & Ferguson have applied principles of Gothic massing. Indeed, one's eye is intrigued by the varied planes of the facade.

Inside, Cram, Goodhue & Ferguson spared no expense, echoing some of the best examples of American Arts and Crafts styling. Dark stained

Quarters

Quarters interior

oak paneling and wainscotting are in abundance. The entry vestibule is a rich, wooden space that leads, on oak flooring, into a larger open space that acts as a reception area. From this area, one can move easily into the front parlor, the library, or the dining room. Movement through the house is easy because of the open plan downstairs; upstairs, the bedroom level has staggered doors and is more private.

Every parlor, library, and dining room in the houses has a fireplace. These vary from house to house, some brick, some terracotta. The dining-room mantle in house #122 is a floor-to-ceiling affair, all in matching wood, with deep moldings. Throughout the house are an abundance of other touches. A bay window offers a nice window seat; there are also window seats on the stair-landings. Leaded-glass is used on some exterior windows and some bookcases (often on the mantels or flanking the fireplaces). Each house has a unique baluster style, which is repeated on the cover of the hall radiator cover.

These houses represent some of the most meticulous work of Cram, Goodhue & Ferguson, and it is to their credit that they were able to give as much detail to mere housing as they did to some of their larger buildings. Certainly, the Academy has recognized the value of these homes and has preserved them and their environs. (The homes will be under going renovations during the next few years.)

38. Cemetery Chapel (#689)

Architect unknown, possibly Richard Delafield, 1837

> The practice of obligatory cadet Sunday worship is almost as old as
> the Military Academy itself. Prior to the appointment of the first official
> chaplain in August, 1813, visiting clergymen or the superintendent con-
> ducted services. The first chaplain, the Reverend Adam Empie, also
> served as Professor of Geography, History, and Ethics. Moreover he per-
> formed the additional duties of treasurer of the Military Academy from
> 1815 to 1816. There being no chapel at West Point, services were con-
> ducted in the mess hall, in class rooms, or, occasionally, out of doors.
>
> —George S. Pappas, *The Cadet Chapel*

In 1829 the issue of a permanent chapel for the Academy was addressed by
the board of visitors. Plans were discussed and in 1833 Congress appropriated $10,000 for construction. The building, originally located prominently
next to the Old Library on the Plain, is typical of the Greek Revival style,

Cemetery Chapel

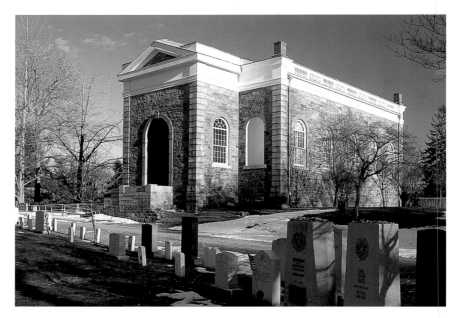

Cemetery Chapel, rear

Cemetery Chapel, interior

albeit a very early example. Four Doric columns and Doric pilasters adorn and support the Roman-style porch (there is a second porch on the rear of the building). The building features canonical Doric details, with, for example, metopes and mutules on the entablature and a heavy cornice. There is even a substantial balustrade along the roof. Entirely of granite, the walls and foundation present a rugged and masculine exterior, in keeping with the traditions of the Doric style.

Inside, where most of the changes have been merely decorative, the visitor will discover a host of significant features. Stenciling, which may be original, adorns the walls. Above the altar is the mural *War and Peace*, painted by Professor of Drawing Robert Weir in 1840. (Weir is also responsible for the decorations of the Episcopal church, Holy Innocents, in Highland Falls, as well as the painting *Embarkation of the Pilgrims* in the rotunda of the Capitol in Washington, D.C.) Flanking the altar are eighteen-foot-tall wooden Corinthian columns. Cushions on the pews and curtains were first installed in 1841 (and have been changed over the years). In 1859 the first money was collected toward memorial plaques, which are now scattered over the walls. The visitor will want to seek out that of Benedict Arnold. He is honored for his fighting against the British, but his plaque states only his rank and date of birth in order to show his dishonor for trying to turn over West Point to the British while he served as commanding officer at West Point. All that is presented is: "Major General—Born 1740." Many other well-known names can be found among the plaques. Under the central aisle of the chapel was situated a special lift to use for mortuary purposes; if the deceased perished during the winter months, the casket would be lowered down into the crypt and kept there until the cemetery ground thawed in the spring.

Of course, like all else at the Point, the Academy outgrew the chapel. By 1899 there was discussion of enlarging the building; however, in the 1903 competition provision was made for an entirely new chapel. Slated for destruction, the original chapel was saved from demolition by

Cemetery

Old Academy gates

public outcry. In 1910 it was moved, stone by stone, to its new and present location, at the southern end of the cemetery. This end had previously held a vegetable garden for most of the nineteenth century. On June 12, 1910, the last official chapel service was held here and a new hymn was introduced. Chaplain Reverend Herbert Shipman wrote the words and W. Franke Harling wrote the music for "The Corps," the song that would become the hymn of the Corps of Cadets.

To visit the chapel one must pass through the nineteenth-century iron gates. Once in the precinct, visitors will certainly want to peruse the

Custer monument

cemetery itself. Herein are a wealth of memorials and monuments to such notables as Margaret "Molly" Corbin, who fought in the Revolutionary War after her husband fell; Civil War Major General Daniel Butterfield, author of "Taps"; General George A. Custer (who graduated bottom of his class at the Academy); Edward White, the first man to walk in space; and George W. Goethals, builder of the Panama Canal. Note also the Egyptian-style mausoleum designed by and containing the remains of General Egbert C. Viele. Viele was so terrified of being buried alive that he designed his own mausoleum with an alarm system.

Cadet Monument, 1818; Norris V. Kain, sculptor

The board of visitors, writing in its report of 1904, recognized the value and meaning of the chapel and the new role it would have on the campus:

> It is understood that the Chapel, with its famous treasures and relics, reminding us of olden times and the heroic deeds of the Army, its officers and men, from the infancy of the Republic until the present day, will be retained, through the building itself must be removed from its present location. The Board cannot too strongly urge that every feature of this historical structure and the contents shall be reproduced and preserved as a precious reminder of the past and a valued legacy for the future.

Enlisted Area Housing

All of the homes in this area were constructed prior to the 1960s (when a new housing development was begun to the southwest), and many were built during the nineteenth century. Individually, most of the houses in this area are not of tremendous architectural significance but are of historic interest. They represent fine examples of base planning by (mainly) the army quartermaster's office. They also reflect some of the changes in American house design over many decades. (Note: many of the house designs are repeated throughout the area.)

39. Enlisted Men's Family Quarters (#344)

Office of the Quartermaster, c. 1890

This duplex house was constructed later than most of the surrounding homes and represents a continuing effort to separate the Enlisted Men's Area from the Academy. At one time many houses in this style lined the streets of this area.

40. Enlisted Men's Family Quarters (#352)

Office of the Quartermaster, c. 1865

Smaller than later quarters, these vernacular frame houses were originally designated for non-commissioned officers. They are duplex homes with a kitchen and living area downstairs and two bedrooms and bath upstairs.

41. Enlisted Men's Family Quarters (#374)

Office of the Quartermaster, 1894

Tall and narrow, and Greek cross in plan, this house was built as the Hospital Steward's Quarters. Similar to the Steward's Quarters built at Fort Porter, New York, this design was not an uncommon plan for military housing of the period. Alterations to the exterior include the additions of a rear bath and porch and the north portion of the front porch in 1901. The orange-brick exterior retains most of its original finishes.

Enlisted Men's Family Quarters (#374)

Enlisted Men's Family Quarters

42. Enlisted Men's Family Quarters (#126)

Office of the Quartermaster, 1891

This building was constructed as the hospital for enlisted men. In 1890 significant effort and money were spent on improving the Enlisted Men's Area. This effort culminated with the construction of the eagerly awaited hospital. It was to be situated in a central location, on a hillock between sites of two older vegetable gardens—an elevated location that provided fresh air and proper sewage run-off.

The building was typical of a very standard sort of military hospital plan built across America on many different bases. A two-story center section, much like a Federal-style house, rose above one-story wings. The center section housed the required storerooms as well as the kitchen, dispensary, mess, operating rooms, isolation rooms, and labs. The wings contained the wards with twelve beds each, and underneath, in the basement, the morgues. An expansive porch wraps around most of the building at the first floor level. The porch, which would have encouraged open-air recuperation, is a typical feature for hospitals and asylums of this period.

Situated between the Enlisted Men's Area and the Academic Area, the hospital aided the growing separation of these areas. While the hospital was a useful and much needed building, like everything else at West Point, it was quickly outgrown. A 1909 board of visitors report complained that "a semi-modern building of 24 beds" was hardly suitable for the more than 700 enlisted men and civilian employees of the base. With the construction of a new hospital, this original building became a military police barracks for a short while, and in 1936 underwent larger interior modifications to become three Officer's Quarters. It now functions as housing for enlisted men and their families.

Religious Education Facility

43. Religious Education Facility (#692) *Architect unknown, 1887*

This house was one of several built as quarters for enlisted men. It was part of the expansion that occurred around the time of construction of the Enlisted Men's Hospital.

44. Switch Station (#715) *Architect unknown, 1867*

Although an unremarkable building this switch station was originally the Small Arms Pyro Magazine. It remains today, on the outside, almost exactly as it was when constructed in 1867. The strong steel door is original.

45. Post Chapel (#799) *Office of the Quartermaster, 1943*

By the turn of the century it was clear that there would be two distinct areas at West Point: the Academy and the Post. Architecturally the separation had been growing for years with the creation of distinct facilities for cadets and enlisted men. In the early 1940s Chief of Staff Colonel Robert C. F. Goetz recognized the need of Post personnel and their families for a place of worship. Plans were received from the quartermaster's office and the Post Chapel was approved. It was dedicated on June 4, 1944.

The building is a standard World War II–era design. It is in a simplified Georgian style. Covered in plain, red brick, this rectangular building is unpretentious and charming: the sash windows are unadorned, the simple belfry is constructed of wood. A slightly projecting tower placed at the entrance breaks up the facade and recalls such notable historic American churches such as Boston's Old North Church and Newport's Trinity Church.

Among the few ornamented exterior details are the hexagonal windows on the corners and the wooden pediment and pilasters at the entrance.

Modifications to the building have been mostly decorative and on the interior. In 1949 wooden window shades were installed and in 1951 new chancel furnishings were donated. The organ, an Aeolian-Skinner, was donated in 1950 by NBC when the room in which it was residing was converted from a radio to a television studio.

In 1952 the simple stained glass windows were donated and began to be installed. They portray "George Washington at Valley Forge," "The Brotherhood of Man," "The First Protestant Communion," "Lincoln's Inaugural Address," "Roger Williams, Apostle to the Indians," "The Risen Christ," and "The Four Chaplains"— the last commemorating those ministers who gave up their seats on the lifeboats when the *USS Dorchester* sank during World War II.

Post Chapel, Four Chaplains window

Post Chapel

Post Services Area

46 | Fire and Emergency Services Administration

47 | Quarters

48 | Community Center

49 | Ordinance Compound

50 | Intercollegiate Athletics

51 | Eisenhower Hall

52 | Gillis Field House

53 | Rifle and Pistol Range

54 | Old Main Guard House and Dunstan Buildings

55 | Director of Housing and Public Works

56 | Military Police Building

57 | Band Barracks / Post Exchange and Cadet Store

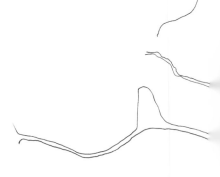

CEMETERY

HARDEE PLACE

WASHINGTON RD

(57)

(56)

(54)

(53)

(46)

(55)

NORTH
ATHLETIC
FIELD

UPTON RD

HUDSON RIVER

TOWER RD

(52)

RUGER RD

(51)

PITCHER RD

(48)

(47)

HOWARD RD

(50)

(49)

CULLUM RD

PARADE GROUND

Where Academy and Army Meet

Situated essentially between the cadet's Academic Area and the Enlisted Men's Area, the Post Services Area is an interesting blend of both. Historically, this area, below the level of the Plain, has been home to some of the more mundane service functions of both Academy and Post. This was due in part to the location of the north dock on the river, which was used for delivery of supplies (unlike the south dock, which was for passengers). Different service needs led to a wide variety of building styles and architectural quality. While the old nineteenth-century laundry that stood here was not an edifice of architectural wonder, the old Band Barracks was a notable, and delightful, structure. Today that remains much the same—the Post Services Area contains buildings of quality and buildings that lack it.

What has changed dramatically, however, is the scale of some of those buildings. Whereas in the nineteenth century, and the first part of the twentieth, the old Bank Barracks was thought large, now there are buildings of a wholly different scale. The Housing and Public Works Building (#667) is a massive building, but Gillis Field House (#663) practically dwarfs it, and it in turn is humbled by the behemoth that is Eisenhower Hall (#655).

The visitor will immediately notice that nearly all of the architecture of this area is executed in brick. This use of a cheaper material reflects the utilitarian nature of most of the buildings located here. Nonetheless, it is fascinating to see in some examples to what good use the simple brick has been put in buildings that are not required to blend in with the Academic Area's granite barracks and classrooms.

Also to the Academy's credit is their use of geography to hide some of the lesser examples of architecture. With only one exception, none of the buildings of the Post Services Area is visible from the Plain. That is, they do not block any views of the Hudson River Valley. The single exception to this is Eisenhower Hall; its grandiose and multifaceted failure boggles the mind.

Walking through the Post Services Area is challenging. There are not many sidewalks and the buildings are quite spread out. It is suggested that the visitor walk through the southern end of the area where the old Ordnance Compound is located and drive through the northern end. This former portion is nearly impossible to enjoy with an automobile, the latter without.

Fire and Emergency Services Administration

46. Fire and Emergency Services Administration (#144)

Architect unknown, 1873

This simple red brick house is notable for its early history as the Band Master's Quarters. It was sited to the north of the old Band Barracks, which was situated in what is now part of Eisenhower Hall's parking lot.

47. Quarters (#146) *Architect unknown, c. 1859*

The history of this tiny cottage is unclear. Records suggest that it was built as a confectionery, but it is known that by 1889 it was being used as quarters by one subaltern. It is also known that the building next door (#147) was, in fact, the boodlers, or confectionery. Some records seem to indicate that this structure may have been a storehouse for the neighboring confectionery. During the late nineteenth century it may have been home to the superintendent of the gas works; in the twentieth century it has been used officer's quarters.

Reflecting many characteristics of the Gothic Revival, the house is very much like a miniature version of the Dean's Quarters (#102) located nearby. Quarters #146 is a symmetrical building with a steep, pointed

Quarters

central gable defining the front. (The porches are a later addition.) Details are typically Gothic Revival, too, with red sandstone hood mouldings over the windows and wooden scrollwork under the eaves. Much as did the Dean's Quarters, this home too must have borrowed from A. J. Downing's design books. (Downing, influential author of Gothic-style residential design books, lived in Newburgh, New York.)

Finally, some visitors might recognize this house from the 1950s motion picture, *The Long Gray Line*. In the film this house was the home of character Marty Mayer.

48. Community Center (#147) *Architect unknown, c. 1878*

No doubt that this small, unobtrusive building had a special place in the hearts of generations of cadets. This was where, for many years, cadets were able to obtain items of great value: confections and tobacco. At West

Point, these items were referred to as "boodle" and thus this shop was affectionately known as the Boodler's Shop or Boodler's.

On this site stood a market and icehouse which burned in 1877. An 1889 inventory of buildings suggests that this current building was built as a one-story replacement in 1878. A report from later that year mentions that the building was to be expanded with a second floor that would include two parlors (one for men and one for ladies), a general waiting room, and two "toilet rooms." The first floor would remain the store. By the end of the century, the building was used as the Cadet Restaurant (not a dining hall), and in 1936 it was converted for use as officers' quarters. The most recent alteration was to convert the interior for use as a community center.

These last two changes utterly altered the interior and some of the windows, but mostly the exterior of the building remains original. It is uncertain if the bricks were always painted or if this was a later modification. (Painting bricks was not uncommon in buildings of this era.) Simple in its execution, the building features a simplified Italianate style enlivened by the dramatic brick cornice and the stone window moulds. Adjacent to the building was, and is, the Ordnance Compound—a rustic, fortress-like granite group of walls and towers. The Boodler's Shop exhibits a very different style, one that is lighter, less serious. This perfectly suited a building that was to offer, for a short time, a break from the rigors of cadet life.

Community Center

49. Ordnance Compound (#635, 635A/B, 637, 671/A)

#635A/B, 637, 671/A: *Attributed to Richard Delafield, c. 1840*

#635: *Attributed to Office of the Quartermaster, c. 1880*

This interesting grouping of smaller buildings is one of the oldest on campus and offers a glimpse into nineteenth-century life at the Academy. Some discrepancies exist in dating, which affect attribution; a few records suggest that construction was begun the year before Richard Delafield's arrival at the Academy. In any case, together with the Old Library and the Old Central Barracks, the Ordnance Compound represents one of the first uses of the rustic Gothic style at West Point. There is more at work in the group of buildings than mere utilitarian functionalism.

Ordnance Compound

Ordnance compound, exterior wall detail

Surrounding the compound are dark granite walls about ten feet tall. The walls are crenellated on all sides and the embrasures and merlons are capped with limestone. At different points in the walls are niches, some of which hold examples of older ordnance. Two gates give access to the compound on the north wall, two on the south. The open area inside the walls held, for many years, war trophies that are now a part of Trophy Point. Forming the northern corners of the wall are similar two-story structures. Building #671 was once named Crozier Hall after Major General William Crozier (Class of 1876), a math instructor. (This is the first of three named buildings in the Ordnance Compound. Each was named and dedicated in 1961.) On the first floor, ammunitions were produced and these were stored on the second. Workers here were kept very busy:

> The routine work at the laboratory by the ordnance detachment includes the care and preservation of all the service and obsolete ordnance, trophy guns, etc., at the post, the preparation of ammunition and blank cartridges for cadet practice and drill, the manufacture of fireworks, and such repairs and other work connected with guns, cartridges, small arms, ammunition, and ordnance supplies generally as may be necessary in the practical instructions of cadets in their various duties.
>
> *—Annual Report* of 1902

Mirroring Crozier Hall is building #671A, Benet Hall, named for Brigadier General Stephen Vincent Benet (Class of 1849), the second head of the department who later served for seventeen years as army chief of ordnance. It most likely housed the office of the instructor of ordnance and gunnery on the first floor and a squadroom for the department of ordnance on the second. Both structures have been heavily modified inside and were at one time barracks for enlisted men and officers. The exteriors, however, are quite original.

On the southern corners are matching two story octagonal towers (#635A and #635B). These rugged ornaments add a great deal to the militaristic style of the compound. Lancet windows on the first floor were later filled in with brick, but it is unclear if these were originally glazed. Although appearing to serve merely as decoration, the towers both served a practical function that could only have been developed at West Point: privy. The first floor room of each was probably originally fitted with a sort of bench seat. It is unknown what the second floor rooms were for but they were accessible via a ladder. Also a mystery is the vent stack on #635B.

Attached to the inside of the northern wall of the compound is a house-sized, two-story granite building (#637). This building was once called Benton Hall after Colonel James G. Benton (Class of 1842), the first instructor and head of the then department of ordnance and science of gunnery. It served as a storage facility for some period of time and then as barracks for the ordnance detachment from 1913 to 1947, even though the teaching of ordnance moved to the East Academic Building in 1913. Enlisted men lived here after 1947. Now it functions as a location for the Cadet Activity Club.

The building has been heavily modified inside and out yet still maintains its distinct appearance. Entrances have been cut, or filled in, and steps on the second floor have been removed, giving the building a very awkward appearance. Still, with its brownstone mouldings and slip sills, its daring turrets and crenellations, it manages to impress the viewer with its rocky strength.

In almost the middle of the compound is a freestanding, one-story brick building (#635). Built around 1880 this brick building represents a more utilitarian structure which, sadly, was placed in the middle of the Ordnance Compound. It was a blacksmith/carpenter/paint shop until converted for use as barracks in 1939. In 1947 the signal corps took over and altered the building so it would be suitable for the viewing and storage of films, and a final alteration in 1957 created a space for cadet recreation.

50. Intercollegiate Athletics (#639)   *Paul Cret, 1937*

Constructed of red brick, reinforced concrete, and limestone trim, Cret's building was originally home to the ordnance and engineering laboratories. The building is clearly not up to the standards of Cret or the Academic Area granite buildings, but it functions in a secondary role and is not visible from the Plain.

Primarily a long rectangular building, it was designed in rather a modernist mode but with some nods to the rustic Gothic traditions of the Academy. The massing is simple, as is the ornament. Cret breaks up the long facade with a repeating group of windows divided by stylized buttresses and with a squat tower down toward the east end. Limestone trim helps enliven the tower, but it is odd that Cret did not use this stone to designate an entrance. Instead, the main entrance on this side is on the west end of the facade. Still extant here are the diagonally paneled doors with metal strap hinges.

Given the dates of Cret's work and the fact that it was not to be one of the Academy's premier buildings, one may excuse the stylistic excursion.

Intercollegiate Athletics

However, when compared to the Post Services Area work of Quartermaster Edwin V. Dunstan, completed about the same time, it is evident that lower cost, utilitarian buildings can indeed contribute to the overall stylistic scheme of the Academy.

51. Eisenhower Hall (#655)   *Welton Becket & Associates, 1974*

> One of the last major buildings constructed at West Point, this was built in 1974, and led to the demolition of several historic buildings. This building contains no positive architectural or historical values at this time. Its location and style obstruct the vista between the Plain and the river to the north.
>
> —*Historic American Buildings Survey: West Point*, 1981

There are two grand instances of betrayal at the United States Military Academy at West Point. The betrayals are similar in this regard: they were committed by those who knew West Point well and had been associated with it intimately. The first was that of Benedict Arnold who attempted, and failed, to weaken West Point's forts enough to allow the British an easy victory. The second was the construction of Eisenhower Hall.

It is difficult to imagine the amount of shortsightedness that allowed a structure as awful as Eisenhower Hall to be built. And, of course, it is not merely that the building is bad that disturbs one so but that, after so many years of careful planning and protection, it was allowed to rise sufficiently above the level of the Plain to block a portion of the river view. To add insult to injury, a number of nineteenth-century buildings, including the historic, 100-year-old Band Barracks, were razed to make room.

Eisenhower Hall

Old Band Barracks. Built 1870s; demolished 1970

Eisenhower Hall is an impressive building in a statistical sense. It is 395 feet long and 200 feet wide, with a variety of heights as it is built into the hillside. Constructed of 1.6 million bricks, it requires 800 tons of air-conditioning equipment to cool it. Inside is 192,000 square feet of floor space. There is a restaurant and a ballroom, each of which can accommodate one thousand people. The auditorium is large enough to host Broadway plays. Some 4,500 seats are available in the auditorium; this is the only building on the entire campus where the entire Corps of Cadets can be seated.

There had been plans for a huge theater on this location as early as 1943—only back then they needed room for merely three thousand. As one may imagine, it took many years to obtain the $26 million necessary to construct Eisenhower Hall. One might wish the Academy had spent an equally significant amount of time siting the building.

52. Gillis Field House (#663)   *Paul Cret, 1937*

Unlike Cret's Ordnance and Engineering Lab (#639) this building seems more on the mark stylistically. It too uses cheaper materials and less ornament but is more sympathetic to the rustic Gothic found in other parts of the campus. This brick structure has random, projecting elements near the top, a stone-capped parapet (with blind gun holes), and interesting molded stone drips at the base of the occasional embrasure.

Decorative brick buttresses adorn the walls. On the gable end of the building is an odd touch: seven recessed multipane windows arranged in vertical rows. These rows seem to be borrowed from P. V. Jensen Klint's Grundvig Church in Copenhagen (1921–26) and are strangely out of place on the Field House.

More appropriate, and more detailed, is the main entrance. It displays a deep, arched portal flanked by two stone towers with stone coping and drips. High above the door in the portal is a carved stone eagle. The door itself is a massive wooden affair with diagonal paneling and iron strap hinges. On the south end is another entrance, this one designated by a squat tower. Distinctive stone brackets below brick arches adorn the space above the arched stone portal. These entrances, along with the side buttresses and parapets lend this building the appropriate stylistic appearance for the Academy and the Post Services Area. That is to say, Cret hit more near the mark with this building, balancing the need for some sense of the Academy's rustic Gothic tradition with the need for a lower cost, more utilitarian building in the Post Services Area.

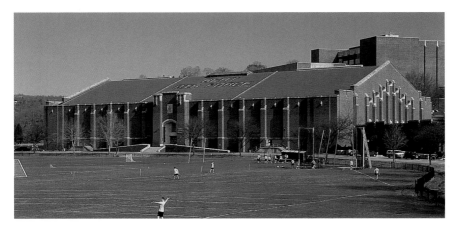

Gillis Field House

Rifle and Pistol Range

53. Rifle and Pistol Range (#665)

Office of the Quartermaster, 1938

This brick building with parapets and buttresses is noted primarily for its adaptation for current use. Designed as essentially a garage, the building was converted for use as a firing range.

54. Old Main Guard House (#675) and Dunstan Buildings

Old Main Guard House   *Architect unknown, c. 1850s*
Dunstan Buildings   *Edwin Dunstan, 1933–1935*

The Main Guard House for this portion of the campus is a simple building. Little is known regarding its history.

Four of the buildings in the northern part of the Post Services Area— #667A/B, 681, 685, 687—were designed by Quartermaster Edwin V. Dunstan. All of them date from the same period, 1933–35. Although the buildings are not visible from the Plain, they are clearly seen from above on Washington Road—indeed, the tower on Building #667 presents such a striking view one might assume that these structures are additional portions of the Academy.

Dunstan thoughtfully designed a sort of brick tribute to the granite and stone buildings by Cram, Goodhue & Ferguson. Rather than merely create a single building, he sought a coherent layout of a series of buildings. In this he was successful. Three of the buildings (#681, 685, 687), placed in a slight curve, relate to one another through geography and siting. Building #667 stands alone, however, and it demonstrates Dunstan's other aim: it echoes, stylistically, the rustic Gothic of the Academic Area buildings.

55. Director of Housing and Public Works (#667A/B)

Edwin Dunstan, 1934

Made up of two sections, A and B, this angled south facade with its seven-story tower and "drawbridge" entrance is the most striking building of the group. The main mass of the structure is five stories tall. Designating the main entrance, the tower has a variety of masses, buttresses, windows, and stone detailing. Crowning the top is a stone parapet; in the center of the top is a carved stone panel of an eagle with spread wings. There are stone shields on the projecting end bays. The entrance is across the drawbridge, through a multipointed Tudor arch.

Director of Housing and Public Works

Military Police Building

56. Military Police Building (#681) *Edwin Dunstan, 1935*

Constructed originally to house the military police, this building features an interesting Y shape. The structure is three stories tall with a fourth story located on the tower at the center of the building. With a variety of differently sized and shaped windows, the contrasting limestone trim, and the central tower, this building is more richly finished than its neighboring counterparts. Located at the base of the tower, the entrance is a dramatic work with diamond-shaped panes in the transom above a multipointed stone arch, and stone lions in relief. The second floor of the wings has an open arcade with stone capped parapets. Appearing as a balcony for the third floor, the space directly above the second-floor arcade is entirely open with a low crenellated parapet at the edge. In other words, the building "steps back" the width of the second floor arcade. The effect of this and the building's shape create a very articulated and dynamic building, one that draws the eye back and forth. Dunstan understood more clearly than some of his better known counterparts how to design a building, with relatively cheap materials, that was interesting and well suited to the campus.

57. Band Barracks / Post Exchange (#685) and Cadet Store (#687)

Band Barracks *Edwin Dunstan, 1933*
Cadet Store, Office and Manufacturing Facilities *Edwin Dunstan, 1935*

These two buildings, similar in appearance, continue and finish the curved plan that Dunstan designed. They are three stories tall with the third story set back, much as in Building #681. Projecting slightly from the center of each of these symmetrical buildings, the center pavilion clearly designates the entrance portal: a pointed stone arch with flanking lions heads in relief. At the top of the central pavilion are three carved panels. The center panel displays a row of flags with eagles at either side. Flanking this panel are two identical panels with stylized displayed eagles.

Cadet Store, Office, and Manufacturing Facilities

WALK SIX

Monuments and Memorials

57 | The Great Chain

58 | Sedgwick Monument

59 | Thayer Monument

60 | Kosciuszko Monument

61 | Battle Monument

62 | Washington Monument

63 | L'École Polytechnique Monument

64 | Patton Monument

65 | Eisenhower Monument

66 | MacArthur Monument

67 | American Soldiers Statue

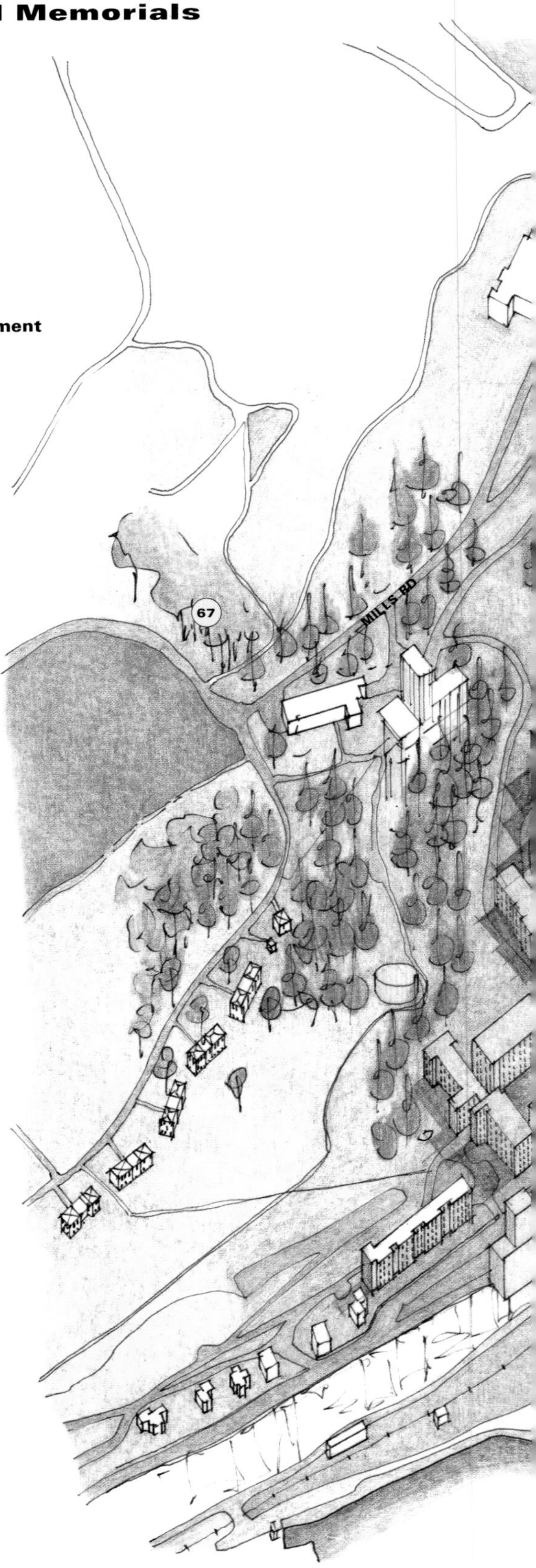

67

MILLS RD

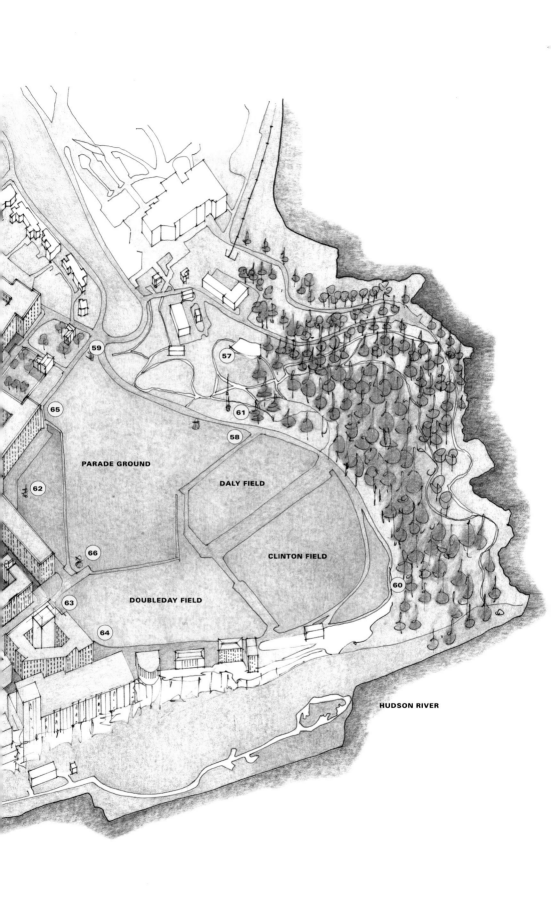

59

57

61

65

58

PARADE GROUND

DALY FIELD

62

CLINTON FIELD

66

60

63

DOUBLEDAY FIELD

64

HUDSON RIVER

Honor and Glory

Across the campus, the visitor will see many monuments and memorials erected to honor alumni and military heroes. These monuments are reverent reminders of America's past and the U.S. military's success in defending the country and its allies. Please take a few moments to pause at each one, to remember and reflect. In addition to those featured in this Walk, others around campus include:

Cadet Monument
  Norris V. Kain, sculptor, 1818
Woods Monument *1824*
Dade Monument *1845*
Margaret Corbin Memorial
  Brython Jones, sculptor, 1926
Sheridan Memorial *1932*
Kelliher-Jobes Memorial *1932*
Wirt Robinson Memorial *1940*
Air Cadet Memorial *1945*
Buckner Memorial *1946*
Victor Constant Memorial *1946*
Class of 1936 Memorial Fountain
  1967
Class of 1957 Memorial Fountain
  1967

Bailey Monument *1973*
Class of 1943 Fountain *1973*
Class of 1933 Clock *1974*
Class of 1943 Fountain *1974*
Class of 1946 Fountain *1974*
Darby Memorial *1974*
Class of 1938 War of Independence
  Monument *1978*
Southeast Asia Memorial *1980*
Class of 1934 Benches *1984*
Flight Memorial *1992*
Buffalo Soldiers *n.d.*
Nike Missile *n.d.*
Battery Sherburne Monument
  n.d.

58. Sedgwick Monument

L. Thompson, 1868

Laurt. Thompson
1868

59. Thayer Monument

C. Conrads, 1883

60. Kosciuszko Monument

Pedestal   *1828, John H. B. Latrobe*
Figure   *1913*

61. Battle Monument

Frederick McMonnies, 1897

62. Washington Monument *Henry Kirk Brown, 1916*

63. L'ÉCOLE Polytechnique Monument *1919*

64. Patton Monument

James E. Fraser, 1950

PRESENTED TO THE CORPS OF CADETS

THE LIVES AND DESTINIES OF VALIANT AMERICA
ARE ENTRUSTED TO YOUR CARE AND LEAD

CLASS OF 1935   CLASS OF

FELIX DE WELDON SCULPTOR 1980

Unpublished Sources (copies in USMA Archives unless otherwise noted)

Building History Record: USMA West Point. Bound record book kept on individual buildings and structures at the Academy, 1929–1943.

Gray, David W. "The Architectural Development of West Point." 1951.

Historic American Buildings Survey Report (HABS NY-5708). (Bethanie C. Grashof, Robie S. Lange, and Travis C. McDonald, authors.) "United States Military Academy, West Point." 1983.

Olmsted Brothers, Landscape Architects. "Report to Accompany General Plans for the United States Military Academy, West Point, New York." 1911.

Olmsted Brothers, Landscape Architects. "Report to Accompany the Preliminary General Plan for the Development of the Landscape of the West Point Military Reservation." August 24, 1906.

"Report of Prof. Charles W. Larned Upon the Reorganization of the Plant of the USMA Accompanied by Estimates, Map and Drawings." 1901.

Stevens, Jim. CPT. "The Delafield Vision: The Architectural Predisposition of USMA to the Tudor-Gothic Style in 1903." 1991.

Published Sources

Ambrose, Stephen. *Duty, Honor, Country: A History of West Point.* Baltimore: Johns Hopkins University Press, 1966.

"American Jews and West Point: The Second Century Priority." West Point Jewish Chapel Fund, n.d. (circa 1977). (Fund-raising booklet, copy in USMA Archives)

Annual Report of the Superintendent of the United States Military Academy. Washington: Government Printing Office, 1904.

Baker, Paul R. *Stanny: The Gilded Life of Stanford White.* New York: The Free Press, 1989.

Baxter, Sylvester. "The New West Point." *The Century Magazine* (July 1904).

Boynton, Brevet Major Edward C. *History of West Point and Its Military Importance During the American Revolution and the Origin and Progress of the United States Military Academy.* New York: D. Van Nostrand, 1863.

Crackei, Theodore J. *The Illustrated History of West Point.* New York: Harry N. Abrams, 1991.

Cram, Ralph Adams. *Church Building: A Study of the Principles of Architecture in their Relation to the Church.* Boston: Small, Maynard & Co., 1914.

———. *My Life in Architecture.* Boston: Little, Brown, 1936.

———. *The Substance of Gothic.* Boston: Marshall Jones, 1925.

Dunstan, Captain Edwin V. "Construction at the Military Academy." *The Quartermaster Review* (November–December 1929).

Guide to West Point. Multiple editions, 1844–1942. These include a wide variety of editions, some official. USMA Archives.

Hills, Edmee J. *The West Point Catholic Experience.* Published by Edmee Hills, 1986. Copy in USMA Archives.

Keezing, Meryl. "Jewish Chapel gets design award." *Newburgh Evening News* (August 4, 1986).

Larned, Colonel Charles W. "The Memorial Hall at West Point." *The Junior Munsey* 4 (July 1900).

Morgan, LTC Brian F., ed. *Bugle Notes 1998.* West Point: USMA, 1998.

Morton, William J., Jr. "A New Wing Added to the Library." *Assembly* 14 (April 1955).

Pappas, George S. *The Cadet Chapel*. West Point: USMA, 1987.

Rogers, Martha. *History of the Post Chapel, West Point, New York*. West Point: USMA, 1964, rev. ed., 1967, 1973.

Reports of Buildings at the USMA: 1888–1900, 1902.

Schuyler, Montgomery. "The Architecture of West Point." *The Architectural Record* 14 (December 1903).

————. "The Works of Cram, Goodhue and Ferguson, A Record of the Firm's Representative Structures, 1892–1910." *Architectural Record* 29 (January 1911).

Turner, Paul V. *Campus: An American Planning Tradition*. Cambridge, Massachusetts: MIT Press, 1984.

White, Theo B. *Paul Philippe Cret, Architect and Teacher*. Cranbury, New Jersey: Associated University Presses, 1973.

No book of this sort is written without the help of a great number of people. The author would particularly like to thank his editor, Jan Cigliano, for her kind encouragement; Dr. William Morgan for his insightful review of the manuscript; and Tish Brewer for her contribution as research assistant. Many people at West Point helped to make the author's job even more delightful. Greg Stegura, Sexton of the Cadet Chapel, provided the author with a private tour of the Cadet Chapel that he will not soon forget. Andrea Hamburger and Debbie DeGraw of the Public Affairs Office helped to open doors and organize tours. Working in the archives was a joy thanks to Susanne Christoff, USMA Archivist, and her pleasant and efficient staff: Sheila Biles, Susan Lintelmann, Alicia Mauldin, and Debbie Pogue. Major Joseph Schafer, Maureen Schafer and their family are most appreciated for their kind hosteling. Finally, the author recognizes the patience and assistance of his wife, Amanda, and daughter, Annika, for accompanying him to New York and listening to his endless chatter about "those West Point buildings."

This research was funded solely by a grant from Hendrix College, to whom the author is even further indebted.

Abramovitz, Max, 81-82
Academic Area, 12-13, 21-23, 25-26, 28-75, 90, 114
Academic Board Room, 40-42
Academy building, 5-6, 74
Adams, John, 5
Administration Building, 16, 35-37, 83
Air Cadet Memorial, 130
Alley, Merle W., 68
American Soldiers Statue, 140
André, John, 4
Arnold, Benedict, 4, 105
Artillery Stables, 19
Arvin Gymnasium, 73-75, 96
Association of Graduates, 63, 90

Bailey Monument, 130
Band Barracks, 114-115, 121-122, 127
Band Master's Quarters, 115
Bartlett, Boyd Wheeler, 52
Bartlett Hall, 32, 38-39, 42, 51-53
Battery Sherburne Monument, 130
Battle Monument, 58, 62, 135
Bellinger, J. B., 22
Benet, Stephen Vincent, 119
Benet Hall, 119
Benton, James G., 120
Benton Hall, 120
Bodley & Garner, 84
Boodler's Shop, 115-117
Bradley, Omar, 18
Bradley Barracks, 8
Branch Exchange, 21
Brown, Henry Kirk, 136
Brunner, Arnold W., 35-37, 42, 68-69
Buckner Memorial, 130
Buffalo Soldiers, 12
Buffalo Soldiers Field, 14, 18-21
Buffalo Soldiers statue, 130
Bush, George, 18
Butterfield, Daniel, 106

Cadet Activity Club, 26-27, 120
Cadet Chapel, 16, 32, 38, 72, 78-79, 82-90
Cadet Guard House, 72
Cadet Mess, 5-6
Cadet Monument, 130
Cadet Restaurant, 117
Cadet Store, 127
Catholic Chapel, 79-81
Catlin, George, 5
Caughy & Evans, 17
Cavalry Barracks, 20
Cavalry Stables, 19

Cemetery Chapel (Old Cadet Chapel), 6, 9, 12, 23, 64, 67, 78, 103-107
Chapels Area, 78-91
Chaplain's Quarters, 89-90
Church, Frederick, 3
Clarke & Rapauno, 68
Class of 1933 Clock, 130
Class of 1934 Benches, 130
Class of 1936 Memorial Fountain, 130
Class of 1938 War of Independence Monument, 130
Class of 1943 Fountain, 130
Class of 1946 Fountain, 130
Class of 1957 Memorial Fountain, 130
Cole, Thomas, 3
Commandant's Quarters, 97
Community Center, 116-117
Company Headquarters and Barracks, 19-20
Conrads, C., 133
Cook, Walter, 31
Corbin, Margaret, 106
Corwin, Daniel, 99
Cram, Goodhue & Ferguson, 8-9, 12, 17, 22, 24, 31-32, 38-39, 42, 47, 51, 53-54, 57, 59, 63-65, 73-74, 83, 89-90, 95-96, 101-102, 124
Cram, Ralph Adams, 8, 26, 31-32, 38-39, 42, 54-58, 79, 84-86
Cram & Goodhue, 24-26
Cret, Paul Philippe, 8, 32-33, 51-53, 65, 72-73, 95-96, 120, 123
Crozier, William, 119
Crozier Hall, 119
Cullum, George W., 60, 78
Cullum Hall (Memorial Hall), 23, 31, 58-64
Cullum Road, 34, 38-39, 52, 56
Custer, George A., 106

Dade Monument, 130
Daly, Leo A., III, 36
Darby Memorial, 130
Davis, Alexander Jackson, 98
Dean's Quarters, 98, 101, 115-116
Delafield, Richard, 6-8, 30-31, 40-41, 47, 49, 66-67, 103, 118
Delano & Aldrich, 33, 56, 68-69, 73
DeRussy, Rene E., 6, 49
Diaper, Frederick, 49
Dougherty, A. E., 26
Downing, Andrew Jackson, 98, 116
Dunstan, Edwin V., 73, 121, 124-127

East Academic Building, 51, 120
Eisenhower, Dwight D., 18

Eisenhower Hall, 8, 66, 73, 114-115, 121-123
Eisenhower Monument, 138
Empie, Adam, 103
Enlisted Men's Area, 94-95, 107-111
Enlisted Men's Hospital, 12,17, 94, 109-111
Enlisted Men's Quarters, 108-109
Enlisted Men's Service Club, 19
Ennis, George Pearse, 71
Ernst, Oswald H., 62-63

Family Housing, 22-26, 100
Fire and Emergency Services Building, 115
Flight Memorial, 130
Ford, Gerald R., 18
Fort Putnam, 95
Four Chaplains window, 111
Fraser, James E., 137

Gardner, Louis, 53
Gehron, William, 68
Gehron & Ross, 42-43, 58
Gehron & Seltzer, 44, 46, 54, 56, 65-66
Gilbert, Cass, 31
Gillis Field House, 114, 123
Gilmore, Q. A., 98
Goethals, George W., 106
Goetz, Robert C. F., 110
Goodhue, Bertram, 18, 83-85, 88-90
Grant, Ulysses S., 3, 17, 78
Grant Barracks, 35
Grant Hall, 42-44, 68
Grashof, Bethanie C., 83
Great Chain, 131
Gymnasium, 63-64, 73-75

Haile Selassie, 89
Hancock, Walter, 139
Harling, W. Franke, 106
Harrison & Abramovitz, 81
Heins & LaFarge, 79
Herbert, James K., 90
Herbert Hall, 90-91
Hospital Steward's Quarters, 108
Housing and Public Works Building, 114, 125
Hudson River, 1-4, 23, 54, 61, 94, 101, 114
Hunt, Richard Morris, 8, 12, 14-16, 31, 42,
    44-47, 53, 63, 74

Intercollegiate Athletics Building, 120-121
Irving, Washington, 17

Jackson, Thomas "Stonewall," 17
Jefferson, Thomas, 5-6, 41
Jewish Chapel, 81-82
Johnson, Tom Lofton, 70-71
Jones, Brython, 130

Kain, Norris V., 107, 130

Kelliher-Jobes Memorial, 130
Kennedy, John F., 18
Klint, P. V. Jensen, 123
Kosciuszko Monument, 134
Kosciuszko's Garden, 61

Lady Cliff College, 12-14, 16, 23
Larned, Charles W., 31-32, 46, 53, 63, 74
Latrobe, Benjamin H., 6
Latrobe, John H. B., 134
Lawrie, Lee, 40, 42, 85
L'École Polytechnique Monument, 137
Lee, Robert E., 3, 17
Lee Barracks, 35, 37-38
Lee Hall, 40-42
Library. *See* Old Library; USMA Library
Lincoln Hall, 63-65
Littlejohn, Robert M., 14-15
Lusk Reservoir, 90

MacArthur, Douglas, 3, 18, 50, 71
MacArthur Monument, 139
Mahan, Dennis Hart, 35
Mahan Hall, 34-35, 38
Margaret Corbin Memorial, 130
McKim, Charles, 63
McKim, Mead & White, 8, 23, 31, 58-64
McMonnies, Frederick, 135
Memorial Hall. *See* Cullum Hall
Meneely Bell Company, 89
Military Peace Establishment Act, 5
Military Police Building, 126
Mills, Robert, 31
Monroe, James, 41
Mongitore, James, 68
Moore, Stephen, 5
Museum, 13-14, 40

New South Barracks, 42-44
Nike Missile monument, 130
Nixon, Richard M., 18
North Barracks, 5-6, 16

O'Connor & Kilham, 33-34, 37-38, 68-70
Officers' Mess, 31, 58-59, 64
Officers' Quarters, 21-26, 58, 63, 100-102
O'Keefe, C. G., 79-80
Old Cadet Chapel. *See* Cemetery Chapel
Old Central Barracks, 8, 30, 48-50, 64, 118
Old Library, 6-9, 23, 30, 49, 51-52, 64, 66-67,
    103, 118
Old Main Guard House, 124
Old Observatory, 80
Olmsted, Frederick Law, 86
Olmsted, George H., 14
Olmsted Hall, 13-14
Ordnance Compound, 7, 16, 30, 47, 49, 114,
    117-120

Ordnance and Engineering Lab, 123
Ordnance Museum, 40

Pappas, George S., 103
Patton, George S., 3, 50
Patton Monument, 137
Pennell, William F., 68
Pershing, John J., 3, 50
Pershing Barracks, 8, 15, 35, 42, 44-47, 53, 74
Pershing Center, 13-14
Plain, 6, 9, 12-13, 17, 30-33, 47, 58, 61, 63-64,
    67, 70-73, 83-84, 90, 94, 96, 103, 114, 121,
    124
Poe, Edgar Allan, 17
Post, George B., 31
Post Chapel, 78, 110-111
Post Exchange, 127
Post Library, 19
Post Services Area, 114-127
Power House, 57-58
Proctor, Arthur B., 19-20
Professors' Row, 99
Provost Marshall's Office, 20-21

Quarters, 115-116
Quinlivan, Pierik & Krause, 90

Railroad station, 26-27
Raymond & Rado, 73
Register of Officers and Graduates, 60
Religious Education Facility, 110
Revolutionary War, 3-5, 105-106, 121
Riding Hall, 12, 56-57
Rifle and Pistol Range, 124
Roe–Eliseo, 14
Rogers, Isaiah, 49
Roosevelt, Theodore, 12
Ross, Albert, 62
Ross, Sidney F., 68
Ruskin, John, 3

Sasaki Associates, 73, 75
Schofield, John M., 31
Schuyler, Montgomery, 38
Scott, Winfield, 17
Scott Barracks, 32, 72-73
Sedgwick Monument, 132
Sentry Station, 14-16
Sheridan Memorial, 130
Sherman, William Tecumseh, 3, 17
Sherman Barracks, 37-38
Shipman, Herberty, 106
Simon, Sidney, 82
Small Arms Pyro Magazine, 110
Soldiers Club, 21

South Barracks, 5-6
Southeast Asia Memorial, 130
Spanish-American War, 12, 62
Superintendent's Office, 42
Superintendent's Quarters, 95-97
Sverdrup & Parcell, 73
Swift, Joseph G., 40, 78
Switch Station, 110

Taylor Hall, 38-42, 54, 57, 74
Thayer, Sylvanus, 17, 23, 40, 48, 56, 78, 95
Thayer Bridge, 39
Thayer Gate, 13-16
Thayer Hall, 18, 38, 54-57
Thayer Hotel, 17-18
Thayer Monument, 133
Thayer Road, 12, 14, 21-22, 24, 35-38, 42, 51, 53
Thompson, L., 132
Totten, Joseph G., 40
Trophy Point, 17

Upton, Emory, 78
USMA Library, 65-67

Vaughan, Henry, 84
Victor Constant Memorial, 130
Viele, Egbert C., 106
Visitor Center, 13-14, 20

Wanamaker, John, 63
War of 1812, 62, 94
Washington, George, 4-5, 40, 71
Washington Hall, 33, 47, 68-71, 73, 84, 96
Washington Monument, 68, 136
Washington Road, 21, 94
Water Treatment Plant, 82-83
Weir, Robert, 105
Weldon, Felix de, 140
Welton Becket & Associates, 121
West Point Club, 58-59
West Point Hotel, 17-18
Whistler, James McNeill, 17
White, Edward, 106
White, Stanford, 32, 58-59, 62
Willet Stained Glass Company, 86
Williams, Jonathan, 40
Wilson, Superintendent, 45
Wilson Road, 21-22
Wirt Robinson Memorial, 130
Wisdopf & Pickworth, 68
Wood Monument, 5, 130
World War I, 87
World War II, 16, 111

York & Sawyer, 35